FREE Study Skills DVD Offer

Dear Customer,

Thank you for your purchase from Mometrix! We consider it an honor and a privilege that you have purchased our product and we want to ensure your satisfaction.

As a way of showing our appreciation and to help us better serve you, we have developed a Study Skills DVD that we would like to give you for FREE. This DVD covers our *best practices* for getting ready for your exam, from how to use our study materials to how to best prepare for the day of the test.

All that we ask is that you email us with feedback that would describe your experience so far with our product. Good, bad, or indifferent, we want to know what you think!

To get your FREE Study Skills DVD, email freedvd@mometrix.com with *FREE STUDY SKILLS DVD* in the subject line and the following information in the body of the email:

- The name of the product you purchased.
- Your product rating on a scale of 1-5, with 5 being the highest rating.
- Your feedback. It can be long, short, or anything in between. We just want to know your impressions and experience so far with our product. (Good feedback might include how our study material met your needs and ways we might be able to make it even better. You could highlight features that you found helpful or features that you think we should add.)
- Your full name and shipping address where you would like us to send your free DVD.

If you have any questions or concerns, please don't hesitate to contact me directly.

Thanks again!

Sincerely,

Jay Willis
Vice President
jay.willis@mometrix.com
1-800-673-8175

ACCUPLACER

SECRETS

Study Guide
Your Key to Exam Success

Written and edited by the Mometrix College Placement Test Team

Printed in the United States of America

This paper meets the requirements of ANSI/NISO Z39.48-1992 (Permanence of Paper).

Mometrix offers volume discount pricing to institutions. For more information or a price quote, please contact our sales department at sales@mometrix.com or 888-248-1219.

Paperback
ISBN 13: 978-1-62733-518-8
ISBN 10: 1-62733-518-8

Ebook
ISBN 13: 978-1-62120-283-7
ISBN 10: 1-62120-283-6

Hardback
ISBN 13: 978-1-5167-0535-1
ISBN 10: 1-5167-0535-1

DEAR FUTURE EXAM SUCCESS STORY

First of all, **THANK YOU** for purchasing Mometrix study materials!

Second, congratulations! You are one of the few determined test-takers who are committed to doing whatever it takes to excel on your exam. **You have come to the right place.** We developed these study materials with one goal in mind: to deliver you the information you need in a format that's concise and easy to use.

In addition to optimizing your guide for the content of the test, we've outlined our recommended steps for breaking down the preparation process into small, attainable goals so you can make sure you stay on track.

We've also analyzed the entire test-taking process, identifying the most common pitfalls and showing how you can overcome them and be ready for any curveball the test throws you.

Standardized testing is one of the biggest obstacles on your road to success, which only increases the importance of doing well in the high-pressure, high-stakes environment of test day. Your results on this test could have a significant impact on your future, and this guide provides the information and practical advice to help you achieve your full potential on test day.

Your success is our success

We would love to hear from you! If you would like to share the story of your exam success or if you have any questions or comments in regard to our products, please contact us at **800-673-8175** or **support@mometrix.com**.

Thanks again for your business and we wish you continued success!

Sincerely,
The Mometrix Test Preparation Team

Need more help? Check out our flashcards at:
http://MometrixFlashcards.com/ACCUPLACER

TABLE OF CONTENTS

Introduction

Thank you for purchasing this resource! You have made the choice to prepare yourself for a test that could have a huge impact on your future, and this guide is designed to help you be fully ready for test day. Obviously, it's important to have a solid understanding of the test material, but you also need to be prepared for the unique environment and stressors of the test, so that you can perform to the best of your abilities.

For this purpose, the first section that appears in this guide is the **Secret Keys**. We've devoted countless hours to meticulously researching what works and what doesn't, and we've boiled down our findings to the four most impactful steps you can take to improve your performance on the test. We start at the beginning with study planning and move through the preparation process, all the way to the testing strategies that will help you get the most out of what you know when you're finally sitting in front of the test.

We recommend that you start preparing for your test as far in advance as possible. However, if you've bought this guide as a last-minute study resource and only have a few days before your test, we recommend that you skip over the first two Secret Keys since they address a long-term study plan.

If you struggle with **test anxiety**, we strongly encourage you to check out our recommendations for how you can overcome it. Test anxiety is a formidable foe, but it can be beaten, and we want to make sure you have the tools you need to defeat it.

1

Secret Key #1 – Plan Big, Study Small

There's a lot riding on your performance. If you want to ace this test, you're going to need to keep your skills sharp and the material fresh in your mind. You need a plan that lets you review everything you need to know while still fitting in your schedule. We'll break this strategy down into three categories.

Information Organization

Start with the information you already have: the official test outline. From this, you can make a complete list of all the concepts you need to cover before the test. Organize these concepts into groups that can be studied together, and create a list of any related vocabulary you need to learn so you can brush up on any difficult terms. You'll want to keep this vocabulary list handy once you actually start studying since you may need to add to it along the way.

Time Management

Once you have your set of study concepts, decide how to spread them out over the time you have left before the test. Break your study plan into small, clear goals so you have a manageable task for each day and know exactly what you're doing. Then just focus on one small step at a time. When you manage your time this way, you don't need to spend hours at a time studying. Studying a small block of content for a short period each day helps you retain information better and avoid stressing over how much you have left to do. You can relax knowing that you have a plan to cover everything in time. In order for this strategy to be effective though, you have to start studying early and stick to your schedule. Avoid the exhaustion and futility that comes from last-minute cramming!

Study Environment

The environment you study in has a big impact on your learning. Studying in a coffee shop, while probably more enjoyable, is not likely to be as fruitful as studying in a quiet room. It's important to keep distractions to a minimum. You're only planning to study for a short block of time, so make the most of it. Don't pause to check your phone or get up to find a snack. It's also important to **avoid multitasking**. Research has consistently shown that multitasking will make your studying dramatically less effective. Your study area should also be comfortable and well-lit so you don't have the distraction of straining your eyes or sitting on an uncomfortable chair.

The time of day you study is also important. You want to be rested and alert. Don't wait until just before bedtime. Study when you'll be most likely to comprehend and remember. Even better, if you know what time of day your test will be, set that time aside for study. That way your brain will be used to working on that subject at that specific time and you'll have a better chance of recalling information.

Finally, it can be helpful to team up with others who are studying for the same test. Your actual studying should be done in as isolated an environment as possible, but the work of organizing the information and setting up the study plan can be divided up. In between study sessions, you can discuss with your teammates the concepts that you're all studying and quiz each other on the details. Just be sure that your teammates are as serious about the test as you are. If you find that your study time is being replaced with social time, you might need to find a new team.

Secret Key #2 – Make Your Studying Count

You're devoting a lot of time and effort to preparing for this test, so you want to be absolutely certain it will pay off. This means doing more than just reading the content and hoping you can remember it on test day. It's important to make every minute of study count. There are two main areas you can focus on to make your studying count:

Retention

It doesn't matter how much time you study if you can't remember the material. You need to make sure you are retaining the concepts. To check your retention of the information you're learning, try recalling it at later times with minimal prompting. Try carrying around flashcards and glance at one or two from time to time or ask a friend who's also studying for the test to quiz you.

To enhance your retention, look for ways to put the information into practice so that you can apply it rather than simply recalling it. If you're using the information in practical ways, it will be much easier to remember. Similarly, it helps to solidify a concept in your mind if you're not only reading it to yourself but also explaining it to someone else. Ask a friend to let you teach them about a concept you're a little shaky on (or speak aloud to an imaginary audience if necessary). As you try to summarize, define, give examples, and answer your friend's questions, you'll understand the concepts better and they will stay with you longer. Finally, step back for a big picture view and ask yourself how each piece of information fits with the whole subject. When you link the different concepts together and see them working together as a whole, it's easier to remember the individual components.

Finally, practice showing your work on any multi-step problems, even if you're just studying. Writing out each step you take to solve a problem will help solidify the process in your mind, and you'll be more likely to remember it during the test.

Modality

Modality simply refers to the means or method by which you study. Choosing a study modality that fits your own individual learning style is crucial. No two people learn best in exactly the same way, so it's important to know your strengths and use them to your advantage.

For example, if you learn best by visualization, focus on visualizing a concept in your mind and draw an image or a diagram. Try color-coding your notes, illustrating them, or creating symbols that will trigger your mind to recall a learned concept. If you learn best by hearing or discussing information, find a study partner who learns the same way or read aloud to yourself. Think about how to put the information in your own words. Imagine that you are giving a lecture on the topic and record yourself so you can listen to it later.

For any learning style, flashcards can be helpful. Organize the information so you can take advantage of spare moments to review. Underline key words or phrases. Use different colors for different categories. Mnemonic devices (such as creating a short list in which every item starts with the same letter) can also help with retention. Find what works best for you and use it to store the information in your mind most effectively and easily.

Secret Key #3 – Practice the Right Way

Your success on test day depends not only on how many hours you put into preparing, but also on whether you prepared the right way. It's good to check along the way to see if your studying is paying off. One of the most effective ways to do this is by taking practice tests to evaluate your progress. Practice tests are useful because they show exactly where you need to improve. Every time you take a practice test, pay special attention to these three groups of questions:

- The questions you got wrong
- The questions you had to guess on, even if you guessed right
- The questions you found difficult or slow to work through

This will show you exactly what your weak areas are, and where you need to devote more study time. Ask yourself why each of these questions gave you trouble. Was it because you didn't understand the material? Was it because you didn't remember the vocabulary? Do you need more repetitions on this type of question to build speed and confidence? Dig into those questions and figure out how you can strengthen your weak areas as you go back to review the material.

Additionally, many practice tests have a section explaining the answer choices. It can be tempting to read the explanation and think that you now have a good understanding of the concept. However, an explanation likely only covers part of the question's broader context. Even if the explanation makes sense, **go back and investigate** every concept related to the question until you're positive you have a thorough understanding.

As you go along, keep in mind that the practice test is just that: practice. Memorizing these questions and answers will not be very helpful on the actual test because it is unlikely to have any of the same exact questions. If you only know the right answers to the sample questions, you won't be prepared for the real thing. **Study the concepts** until you understand them fully, and then you'll be able to answer any question that shows up on the test.

It's important to wait on the practice tests until you're ready. If you take a test on your first day of study, you may be overwhelmed by the amount of material covered and how much you need to learn. Work up to it gradually.

On test day, you'll need to be prepared for answering questions, managing your time, and using the test-taking strategies you've learned. It's a lot to balance, like a mental marathon that will have a big impact on your future. Like training for a marathon, you'll need to start slowly and work your way up. When test day arrives, you'll be ready.

Start with the strategies you've read in the first two Secret Keys—plan your course and study in the way that works best for you. If you have time, consider using multiple study resources to get different approaches to the same concepts. It can be helpful to see difficult concepts from more than one angle. Then find a good source for practice tests. Many times, the test website will suggest potential study resources or provide sample tests.

Secret Key #4 – Have a Plan for Guessing

When you're taking the test, you may find yourself stuck on a question. Some of the answer choices seem better than others, but you don't see the one answer choice that is obviously correct. What do you do?

The scenario described above is very common, yet most test takers have not effectively prepared for it. Developing and practicing a plan for guessing may be one of the single most effective uses of your time as you get ready for the exam.

In developing your plan for guessing, there are three questions to address:

- When should you start the guessing process?
- How should you narrow down the choices?
- Which answer should you choose?

When to Start the Guessing Process

Unless your plan for guessing is to select C every time (which, despite its merits, is not what we recommend), you need to leave yourself enough time to apply your answer elimination strategies. Since you have a limited amount of time for each question, that means that if you're going to give yourself the best shot at guessing correctly, you have to decide quickly whether or not you will guess.

Of course, the best-case scenario is that you don't have to guess at all, so first, see if you can answer the question based on your knowledge of the subject and basic reasoning skills. Focus on the key words in the question and try to jog your memory of related topics. Give yourself a chance to bring the knowledge to mind, but once you realize that you don't have (or you can't access) the knowledge you need to answer the question, it's time to start the guessing process.

It's almost always better to start the guessing process too early than too late. It only takes a few seconds to remember something and answer the question from knowledge. Carefully eliminating wrong answer choices takes longer. Plus, going through the process of eliminating answer choices can actually help jog your memory.

Summary: Start the guessing process as soon as you decide that you can't answer the question based on your knowledge.

How to Narrow Down the Choices

The next chapter in this book (**Test-Taking Strategies**) includes a wide range of strategies for how to approach questions and how to look for answer choices to eliminate. You will definitely want to read those carefully, practice them, and figure out which ones work best for you. Here though, we're going to address a mindset rather than a particular strategy.

Your chances of guessing an answer correctly depend on how many options you are choosing from.

How many options	Chance to guess correctly
5	20%
4	25%
3	33%
2	50%
1	100%

You can see from this chart just how valuable it is to be able to eliminate incorrect answers and make an educated guess, but there are two things that many test takers do that cause them to miss out on the benefits of guessing:

- Accidentally eliminating the correct answer
- Selecting an answer based on an impression

We'll look at the first one here, and the second one in the next section.

To avoid accidentally eliminating the correct answer, we recommend a thought exercise called **the $5 challenge**. In this challenge, you only eliminate an answer choice from contention if you are willing to bet $5 on it being wrong. Why $5? Five dollars is a small but not insignificant amount of money. It's an amount you could afford to lose but wouldn't want to throw away. And while losing $5 once might not hurt too much, doing it twenty times will set you back $100. In the same way, each small decision you make—eliminating a choice here, guessing on a question there—won't by itself impact your score very much, but when you put them all together, they can make a big difference. By holding each answer choice elimination decision to a higher standard, you can reduce the risk of accidentally eliminating the correct answer.

The $5 challenge can also be applied in a positive sense: If you are willing to bet $5 that an answer choice *is* correct, go ahead and mark it as correct.

Summary: Only eliminate an answer choice if you are willing to bet $5 that it is wrong.

6

Which Answer to Choose

You're taking the test. You've run into a hard question and decided you'll have to guess. You've eliminated all the answer choices you're willing to bet $5 on. Now you have to pick an answer. Why do we even need to talk about this? Why can't you just pick whichever one you feel like when the time comes?

The answer to these questions is that if you don't come into the test with a plan, you'll rely on your impression to select an answer choice, and if you do that, you risk falling into a trap. The test writers know that everyone who takes their test will be guessing on some of the questions, so they intentionally write wrong answer choices to seem plausible. You still have to pick an answer though, and if the wrong answer choices are designed to look right, how can you ever be sure that you're not falling for their trap? The best solution we've found to this dilemma is to take the decision out of your hands entirely. Here is the process we recommend:

Once you've eliminated any choices that you are confident (willing to bet $5) are wrong, select the first remaining choice as your answer.

Whether you choose to select the first remaining choice, the second, or the last, the important thing is that you use some preselected standard. Using this approach guarantees that you will not be enticed into selecting an answer choice that looks right, because you are not basing your decision on how the answer choices look.

This is not meant to make you question your knowledge. Instead, it is to help you recognize the difference between your knowledge and your impressions. There's a huge difference between thinking an answer is right because of what you know, and thinking an answer is right because it looks or sounds like it should be right.

Summary: To ensure that your selection is appropriately random, make a predetermined selection from among all answer choices you have not eliminated.

Test-Taking Strategies

This section contains a list of test-taking strategies that you may find helpful as you work through the test. By taking what you know and applying logical thought, you can maximize your chances of answering any question correctly!

It is very important to realize that every question is different and every person is different: no single strategy will work on every question, and no single strategy will work for every person. That's why we've included all of them here, so you can try them out and determine which ones work best for different types of questions and which ones work best for you.

Question Strategies

READ CAREFULLY

Read the question and answer choices carefully. Don't miss the question because you misread the terms. You have plenty of time to read each question thoroughly and make sure you understand what is being asked. Yet a happy medium must be attained, so don't waste too much time. You must read carefully, but efficiently.

CONTEXTUAL CLUES

Look for contextual clues. If the question includes a word you are not familiar with, look at the immediate context for some indication of what the word might mean. Contextual clues can often give you all the information you need to decipher the meaning of an unfamiliar word. Even if you can't determine the meaning, you may be able to narrow down the possibilities enough to make a solid guess at the answer to the question.

PREFIXES

If you're having trouble with a word in the question or answer choices, try dissecting it. Take advantage of every clue that the word might include. Prefixes and suffixes can be a huge help. Usually they allow you to determine a basic meaning. Pre- means before, post- means after, pro - is positive, de- is negative. From prefixes and suffixes, you can get an idea of the general meaning of the word and try to put it into context.

HEDGE WORDS

Watch out for critical hedge words, such as *likely, may, can, sometimes, often, almost, mostly, usually, generally, rarely,* and *sometimes.* Question writers insert these hedge phrases to cover every possibility. Often an answer choice will be wrong simply because it leaves no room for exception. Be on guard for answer choices that have definitive words such as *exactly* and *always.*

SWITCHBACK WORDS

Stay alert for *switchbacks.* These are the words and phrases frequently used to alert you to shifts in thought. The most common switchback words are *but, although,* and *however.* Others include *nevertheless, on the other hand, even though, while, in spite of, despite, regardless of.* Switchback words are important to catch because they can change the direction of the question or an answer choice.

FACE VALUE

When in doubt, use common sense. Accept the situation in the problem at face value. Don't read too much into it. These problems will not require you to make wild assumptions. If you have to go beyond creativity and warp time or space in order to have an answer choice fit the question, then you should move on and consider the other answer choices. These are normal problems rooted in reality. The applicable relationship or explanation may not be readily apparent, but it is there for you to figure out. Use your common sense to interpret anything that isn't clear.

Answer Choice Strategies

ANSWER SELECTION

The most thorough way to pick an answer choice is to identify and eliminate wrong answers until only one is left, then confirm it is the correct answer. Sometimes an answer choice may immediately seem right, but be careful. The test writers will usually put more than one reasonable answer choice on each question, so take a second to read all of them and make sure that the other choices are not equally obvious. As long as you have time left, it is better to read every answer choice than to pick the first one that looks right without checking the others.

ANSWER CHOICE FAMILIES

An answer choice family consists of two (in rare cases, three) answer choices that are very similar in construction and cannot all be true at the same time. If you see two answer choices that are direct opposites or parallels, one of them is usually the correct answer. For instance, if one answer choice says that quantity x increases and another either says that quantity x decreases (opposite) or says that quantity y increases (parallel), then those answer choices would fall into the same family. An answer choice that doesn't match the construction of the answer choice family is more likely to be incorrect. Most questions will not have answer choice families, but when they do appear, you should be prepared to recognize them.

ELIMINATE ANSWERS

Eliminate answer choices as soon as you realize they are wrong, but make sure you consider all possibilities. If you are eliminating answer choices and realize that the last one you are left with is also wrong, don't panic. Start over and consider each choice again. There may be something you missed the first time that you will realize on the second pass.

AVOID FACT TRAPS

Don't be distracted by an answer choice that is factually true but doesn't answer the question. You are looking for the choice that answers the question. Stay focused on what the question is asking for so you don't accidentally pick an answer that is true but incorrect. Always go back to the question and make sure the answer choice you've selected actually answers the question and is not merely a true statement.

EXTREME STATEMENTS

In general, you should avoid answers that put forth extreme actions as standard practice or proclaim controversial ideas as established fact. An answer choice that states the "process should be used in certain situations, if..." is much more likely to be correct than one that states the "process should be discontinued completely." The first is a calm rational statement and doesn't even make a definitive, uncompromising stance, using a hedge word *if* to provide wiggle room, whereas the second choice is a radical idea and far more extreme.

9

BENCHMARK

As you read through the answer choices and you come across one that seems to answer the question well, mentally select that answer choice. This is not your final answer, but it's the one that will help you evaluate the other answer choices. The one that you selected is your benchmark or standard for judging each of the other answer choices. Every other answer choice must be compared to your benchmark. That choice is correct until proven otherwise by another answer choice beating it. If you find a better answer, then that one becomes your new benchmark. Once you've decided that no other choice answers the question as well as your benchmark, you have your final answer.

PREDICT THE ANSWER

Before you even start looking at the answer choices, it is often best to try to predict the answer. When you come up with the answer on your own, it is easier to avoid distractions and traps because you will know exactly what to look for. The right answer choice is unlikely to be word-for-word what you came up with, but it should be a close match. Even if you are confident that you have the right answer, you should still take the time to read each option before moving on.

General Strategies

TOUGH QUESTIONS

If you are stumped on a problem or it appears too hard or too difficult, don't waste time. Move on! Remember though, if you can quickly check for obviously incorrect answer choices, your chances of guessing correctly are greatly improved. Before you completely give up, at least try to knock out a couple of possible answers. Eliminate what you can and then guess at the remaining answer choices before moving on.

CHECK YOUR WORK

Since you will probably not know every term listed and the answer to every question, it is important that you get credit for the ones that you do know. Don't miss any questions through careless mistakes. If at all possible, try to take a second to look back over your answer selection and make sure you've selected the correct answer choice and haven't made a costly careless mistake (such as marking an answer choice that you didn't mean to mark). This quick double check should more than pay for itself in caught mistakes for the time it costs.

DON'T RUSH

It is very easy to make errors when you are in a hurry. Maintaining a fast pace in answering questions is pointless if it makes you miss questions that you would have gotten right otherwise. Test writers like to include distracting information and wrong answers that seem right. Taking a little extra time to avoid careless mistakes can make all the difference in your test score. Find a pace that allows you to be confident in the answers that you select.

KEEP MOVING

Panicking will not help you pass the test, so do your best to stay calm and keep moving. Taking deep breaths and going through the answer elimination steps you practiced can help to break through a stress barrier and keep your pace.

Final Notes

The combination of a solid foundation of content knowledge and the confidence that comes from practicing your plan for applying that knowledge is the key to maximizing your performance on test day. As your foundation of content knowledge is built up and strengthened, you'll find that the strategies included in this chapter become more and more effective in helping you quickly sift through the distractions and traps of the test to isolate the correct answer.

Now it's time to move on to the test content chapters of this book, but be sure to keep your goal in mind. As you read, think about how you will be able to apply this information on the test. If you've already seen sample questions for the test and you have an idea of the question format and style, try to come up with questions of your own that you can answer based on what you're reading. This will give you valuable practice applying your knowledge in the same ways you can expect to on test day.

Good luck and good studying!

Arithmetic and Elementary Algebra Test

Numbers and Their Classifications

Numbers are the basic building blocks of mathematics. Specific features of numbers are identified by the following terms:

Integers – The set of whole positive and negative numbers, including zero. Integers do not include fractions $\left(\frac{1}{3}\right)$, decimals (0.56), or mixed numbers $\left(7\frac{3}{4}\right)$.

Prime number – A whole number greater than 1 that has only two factors, itself and 1; that is, a number that can be divided evenly only by 1 and itself.

Composite number – A whole number greater than 1 that has more than two different factors; in other words, any whole number that is not a prime number. For example: The composite number 8 has the factors of 1, 2, 4, and 8.

Even number – Any integer that can be divided by 2 without leaving a remainder. For example: 2, 4, 6, 8, and so on.

Odd number – Any integer that cannot be divided evenly by 2. For example: 3, 5, 7, 9, and so on.

Decimal number – a number that uses a decimal point to show the part of the number that is less than one. Example: 1.234.

Decimal point – a symbol used to separate the ones place from the tenths place in decimals or dollars from cents in currency.

Decimal place – the position of a number to the right of the decimal point. In the decimal 0.123, the 1 is in the first place to the right of the decimal point, indicating tenths; the 2 is in the second place, indicating hundredths; and the 3 is in the third place, indicating thousandths.

The decimal, or **base 10**, system is a number system that uses ten different digits (0, 1, 2, 3, 4, 5, 6, 7, 8, 9). An example of a number system that uses something other than ten digits is the binary, or base 2, number system, used by computers, which uses only the numbers 0 and 1. It is thought that the decimal system originated because people had only their 10 fingers for counting.

> **Review Video: <u>Numbers and Their Classifications</u>**
> Visit mometrix.com/academy and enter code: 461071

Rational, irrational, and real numbers can be described as follows:

Rational numbers include all integers, decimals, and fractions. Any terminating or repeating decimal number is a rational number.

> **Review Video: <u>Rational Numbers</u>**
> Visit mometrix.com/academy and enter code: 280645

Irrational numbers cannot be written as fractions or decimals because the number of decimal places is infinite and there is no recurring pattern of digits within the number. For example, pi (π)

begins with 3.141592 and continues without terminating or repeating, so pi is an irrational number.

Review Video: <u>Irrational Numbers on a Number Line</u>
Visit mometrix.com/academy and enter code: 433866

Real numbers are the set of all rational and irrational numbers.

Review Video: <u>Negative and Positive Number Line</u>
Visit mometrix.com/academy and enter code: 816439

Operations

There are four basic mathematical operations:

Addition increases the value of one quantity by the value of another quantity. Example: $2 + 4 = 6; 8 + 9 = 17$. The result is called the **sum**. With addition, the order does not matter. $4 + 2 = 2 + 4$.

Subtraction is the opposite operation to addition; it decreases the value of one quantity by the value of another quantity. Example: $6 - 4 = 2; 17 - 8 = 9$. The result is called the **difference**. Note that with subtraction, the order does matter. $6 - 4 \neq 4 - 6$.

Multiplication can be thought of as repeated addition. One number tells how many times to add the other number to itself. Example: 3×2 (three times two) $= 2 + 2 + 2 = 6$. With multiplication, the order does not matter. $2 \times 3 = 3 \times 2$ or $3 + 3 = 2 + 2 + 2$.

Division is the opposite operation to multiplication; one number tells us how many parts to divide the other number into. Example: $20 \div 4 = 5$; if 20 is split into 4 equal parts, each part is 5. With division, the order of the numbers does matter. $20 \div 4 \neq 4 \div 20$.

An **exponent** is a superscript number placed next to another number at the top right. It indicates how many times the base number is to be multiplied by itself. Exponents provide a shorthand way to write what would be a longer mathematical expression. Example: $a^2 = a \times a; 2^4 = 2 \times 2 \times 2 \times 2$. A number with an exponent of 2 is said to be "*squared*," while a number with an exponent of 3 is said to be "*cubed*." The value of a number raised to an exponent is called its **power**. So, 8^4 is read as "8 to the 4th power," or "8 raised to the power of 4." A **negative exponent** is the same as the reciprocal of a positive exponent. Example: $a^{-2} = \frac{1}{a^2}$.

Parentheses are used to designate which operations should be done first when there are multiple operations. Example: $4 - (2 + 1) = 1$; the parentheses tell us that we must add 2 and 1, and then subtract the sum from 4, rather than subtracting 2 from 4 and then adding 1 (this would give us an answer of 3).

Order of Operations is a set of rules that dictates the order in which we must perform each operation in an expression so that we will evaluate it accurately. If we have an expression that includes multiple different operations, Order of Operations tells us which operations to do first. The most common mnemonic for Order of Operations is **PEMDAS**, or "Please Excuse My Dear Aunt Sally." PEMDAS stands for *Parentheses, Exponents, Multiplication, Division, Addition, Subtraction*. It is important to understand that multiplication and division have equal precedence, as do addition and subtraction, so those pairs of operations are simply worked from left to right in order.

Example: Evaluate the expression $5 + 20 \div 4 \times (2 + 3)^2 - 6$ using the correct order of operations.

P: Perform the operations inside the parentheses, $(2 + 3) = 5$.

E: Simplify the exponents, $(5)^2 = 25$.

The equation now looks like this: $5 + 20 \div 4 \times 25 - 6$.

MD: Perform multiplication and division from left to right, $20 \div 4 = 5$; then $5 \times 25 = 125$.

The equation now looks like this: $5 + 125 - 6$.

AS: Perform addition and subtraction from left to right, $5 + 125 = 130$; then $130 - 6 = 124$.

The laws of exponents are as follows:

1. Any number to the power of 1 is equal to itself: $a^1 = a$.
2. The number 1 raised to any power is equal to 1: $1^n = 1$.
3. Any number raised to the power of 0 is equal to 1: $a^0 = 1$.
4. Add exponents to multiply powers of the same base number: $a^n \times a^m = a^{n+m}$.
5. Subtract exponents to divide powers of the same number; that is $a^n \div a^m = a^{n-m}$.
6. Multiply exponents to raise a power to a power: $(a^n)^m = a^{n \times m}$.
7. If multiplied or divided numbers inside parentheses are collectively raised to a power, this is the same as each individual term being raised to that power: $(a \times b)^n = a^n \times b^n$; $(a \div b)^n = a^n \div b^n$.

Note: Exponents do not have to be integers. Fractional or decimal exponents follow all the rules above as well. Example: $5^{\frac{1}{4}} \times 5^{\frac{3}{4}} = 5^{\frac{1}{4}+\frac{3}{4}} = 5^1 = 5$.

A **root**, such as a *square root*, is another way of writing a fractional exponent. Instead of using a superscript, roots use the radical symbol ($\sqrt{\ }$) to indicate the operation. A radical will have a number underneath the bar, and may sometimes have a number in the upper left: $\sqrt[n]{a}$, read as "the nth root of a." The relationship between radical notation and exponent notation can be described by this equation: $\sqrt[n]{a} = a^{\frac{1}{n}}$.

The two special cases of $n = 2$ and $n = 3$ are called square roots and cube roots. If there is no number to the upper left, it is understood to be a square root ($n = 2$). Nearly all of the roots you encounter will be square roots.

A *square root* is the same as a number raised to the one-half power. When we say that a is the square root of b ($a = \sqrt{b}$), we mean that a multiplied by itself equals b: ($a \times a = b$).

A *perfect square* is a number that has an integer for its square root. There are 10 perfect squares from 1 to 100: 1, 4, 9, 16, 25, 36, 49, 64, 81, 100 (the squares of integers 1 through 10).

Scientific notation is a way of writing large numbers in a shorter form. The form $a \times 10^n$ is used in scientific notation, where a is greater than or equal to 1, but less than 10, and n is the number of places the decimal must move to get from the original number to a. Example: The number 230,400,000 is cumbersome to write. To write the value in scientific notation, place a decimal point between the first and second numbers, and include all digits through the last non-zero digit ($a = 2.304$). To find the appropriate power of 10, count the number of places the decimal point had to move ($n = 8$). The number is positive if the decimal moved to the left, and negative if it moved to the right. We can then write 230,400,000 as 2.304×10^8. If we look instead at the number 0.00002304, we have the same value for a, but this time the decimal moved 5 places to the right ($n = -5$). Thus, 0.00002304 can be written as 2.304×10^{-5}. Using this notation makes it simple to compare very large or very small numbers. By comparing exponents, it is easy to see that 3.28×10^4 is smaller than 1.51×10^5, because 4 is less than 5.

Factors and Multiples

Factors are numbers that are multiplied together to obtain a **product**. For example, in the equation $2 \times 3 = 6$, the numbers 2 and 3 are factors. A prime number has only two factors (1 and itself), but other numbers can have many factors.

A **common factor** is a number that divides exactly into two or more other numbers. For example, the factors of 12 are 1, 2, 3, 4, 6, and 12, while the factors of 15 are 1, 3, 5, and 15. The common factors of 12 and 15 are 1 and 3. A **prime factor** is also a prime number. Therefore, the prime factors of 12 are 2 and 3. For 15, the prime factors are 3 and 5.

> **Review Video: Factors**
> Visit mometrix.com/academy and enter code: 920086

The **greatest common factor** (GCF) is the largest number that is a factor of two or more numbers. For example, the factors of 15 are 1, 3, 5, and 15; the factors of 35 are 1, 5, 7, and 35. Therefore, the greatest common factor of 15 and 35 is 5.

> **Review Video: Greatest Common Factor (GCF)**
> Visit mometrix.com/academy and enter code: 838699

The **least common multiple** (LCM) is the smallest number that is a multiple of two or more numbers. For example, the multiples of 3 include 3, 6, 9, 12, 15, etc.; the multiples of 5 include 5, 10, 15, 20, etc. Therefore, the least common multiple of 3 and 5 is 15.

> **Review Video: Multiples**
> Visit mometrix.com/academy and enter code: 626738
>
> **Review Video: Least Common Multiple**
> Visit mometrix.com/academy and enter code: 946579

Fractions, Percentages, and Related Concepts

A fraction is a number that is expressed as one integer written above another integer, with a dividing line between them $\left(\frac{x}{y}\right)$. It represents the quotient of the two numbers "x divided by y." It can also be thought of as x out of y equal parts.

The top number of a fraction is called the **numerator**, and it represents the number of parts under consideration. The 1 in $\frac{1}{4}$ means that 1 part out of the whole is being considered in the calculation. The bottom number of a fraction is called the **denominator**, and it represents the total number of equal parts. The 4 in $\frac{1}{4}$ means that the whole consists of 4 equal parts. A fraction cannot have a denominator of zero; this is referred to as "*undefined*."

> **Review Video: Fractions**
> Visit mometrix.com/academy and enter code: 262335

Fractions can be **manipulated**, without changing the value of the fraction, by multiplying or dividing (but not adding or subtracting) both the numerator and denominator by the same number. If you divide both numbers by a common factor, you are **reducing** or simplifying the fraction. Two fractions that have the same value, but are expressed differently are known as **equivalent fractions**. For example, $\frac{2}{10}, \frac{3}{15}, \frac{4}{20}$, and $\frac{5}{25}$ are all equivalent fractions. They can also all be reduced or simplified to $\frac{1}{5}$.

When two fractions are manipulated so that they have the same denominator, this is known as finding a **common denominator**. The number chosen to be that common denominator should be the least common multiple of the two original denominators. Example: $\frac{3}{4}$ and $\frac{5}{6}$; the least common multiple of 4 and 6 is 12. Manipulating to achieve the common denominator: $\frac{3}{4} = \frac{9}{12}; \frac{5}{6} = \frac{10}{12}$.

If two fractions have a common denominator, they can be **added** or **subtracted** simply by adding or subtracting the two numerators and retaining the same denominator. Example: $\frac{1}{2} + \frac{1}{4} = \frac{2}{4} + \frac{1}{4} = \frac{3}{4}$. If the two fractions do not already have the same denominator, one or both of them must be manipulated to achieve a common denominator before they can be added or subtracted.

> **Review Video: Adding and Subtracting Fractions**
> Visit mometrix.com/academy and enter code: 378080

Two fractions can be multiplied by **multiplying** the two numerators to find the new numerator and the two denominators to find the new denominator. Example: $\frac{1}{3} \times \frac{2}{3} = \frac{1 \times 2}{3 \times 3} = \frac{2}{9}$.

> **Review Video: Multiplying Fractions**
> Visit mometrix.com/academy and enter code: 638849

Two fractions can be **divided** by flipping the numerator and denominator of the second fraction and then proceeding as though it were a multiplication. Example: $\frac{2}{3} \div \frac{3}{4} = \frac{2}{3} \times \frac{4}{3} = \frac{8}{9}$.

> **Review Video: Dividing Fractions**
> Visit mometrix.com/academy and enter code: 300874

A fraction whose denominator is greater than its numerator is known as a **proper fraction**, while a fraction whose numerator is greater than its denominator is known as an **improper fraction**. Proper fractions have values less than one and improper fractions have values greater than one.

A **mixed number** is a number that contains both an integer and a fraction. Any improper fraction can be rewritten as a mixed number.

Example: $\frac{8}{3} = \frac{6}{3} + \frac{2}{3} = 2 + \frac{2}{3} = 2\frac{2}{3}$. Similarly, any mixed number can be rewritten as an improper fraction. Example: $1\frac{3}{5} = 1 + \frac{3}{5} = \frac{5}{5} + \frac{3}{5} = \frac{8}{5}$.

Percentages can be thought of as fractions that are based on a whole of 100; that is, one whole is equal to 100%. The word percent means "per hundred." Fractions can be expressed as percentages by finding equivalent fractions with a denomination of 100. Example: $\frac{7}{10} = \frac{70}{100} = 70\%$; $\frac{1}{4} = \frac{25}{100} = 25\%$.

To express a percentage as a **fraction**, divide the percentage number by 100 and reduce the fraction to its simplest possible terms. Example: $60\% = \frac{60}{100} = \frac{3}{5}$; $96\% = \frac{96}{100} = \frac{24}{25}$.

Converting **decimals** to percentages and percentages to decimals is as simple as moving the decimal point. To convert from a decimal to a percentage, move the decimal point two places to the right. To convert from a percentage to a decimal, move it two places to the left. Example: 0.23 = 23%; 5.34 = 534%; 0.007 = 0.7%; 700% = 7.00; 86% = 0.86; 0.15% = 0.0015.

It may be helpful to remember that the percentage number will always be larger than the equivalent decimal number.

A percentage problem can be presented three main ways: (1) Find what percentage of some number another number is. Example: What percentage of 40 is 8? (2) Find what number is some percentage of a given number. Example: What number is 20% of 40? (3) Find what number another number is a given percentage of. Example: What number is 8 20% of?

The three components in all of these cases are the same: a **whole** (W), a **part** (P), and a **percentage** (%). These are related by the equation: $P = W \times \%$. This is the form of the equation you would use to solve problems of type (2). To solve types (1) and (3), you would use these two forms: $\% = \frac{P}{W}$ and $W = \frac{P}{\%}$.

The thing that frequently makes percentage problems difficult is that they are most often also **word problems**, so a large part of solving them is figuring out which quantities are what. Example: In a school cafeteria, 7 students choose pizza, 9 choose hamburgers, and 4 choose tacos. Find the percentage that chooses tacos. To find the whole, you must first add all of the parts: 7 + 9 + 4 = 20. The percentage can then be found by dividing the part by the whole ($\% = \frac{P}{W}$): $\frac{4}{20} = \frac{20}{100} = 20\%$.

A **ratio** is a comparison of two quantities in a particular order. Example: If there are 14 computers in a lab, and the class has 20 students, there is a student to computer ratio of 20 to 14, commonly written as 20:14. Ratios are normally reduced to their smallest whole number representation, so 20:14 would be reduced to 10:7 by dividing both sides by 2.

> **Review Video: <u>Ratios</u>**
> Visit mometrix.com/academy and enter code: 996914

A **proportion** is a relationship between two quantities that dictates how one changes when the other changes. A **direct proportion** describes a relationship in which a quantity increases by a set amount for every increase in the other quantity, or decreases by that same amount for every decrease in the other quantity.

Example: Assuming a constant driving speed, the time required for a car trip increases as the distance of the trip increases. The distance to be traveled and the time required to travel are directly proportional.

> **Review Video: <u>Proportions</u>**
> Visit mometrix.com/academy and enter code: 505355

Inverse proportion is a relationship in which an increase in one quantity is accompanied by a decrease in the other, or vice versa. Example: the time required for a car trip decreases as the speed increases, and increases as the speed decreases, so the time required is inversely proportional to the speed of the car.

Polynomial Algebra

Equations are made up of monomials and polynomials. A **monomial** is a single variable or product of constants and variables, such as x, $2x$, or $\frac{2}{x}$. There will never be addition or subtraction symbols in a monomial. Like monomials have like variables, but they may have different coefficients. **Polynomials** are algebraic expressions which use addition and subtraction to combine two or more monomials. Two terms make a binomial, three terms make a trinomial, and so on. The **degree of a monomial** is the sum of the exponents of the variables. The **degree of a polynomial** is the highest degree of any individual term.

> **Review Video: Polynomials**
> Visit mometrix.com/academy and enter code: 305005

To multiply two binomials, follow the *FOIL* method. FOIL stands for:

- **First**: Multiply the first term of each binomial
- **Outer**: Multiply the outer terms of each binomial
- **Inner**: Multiply the inner terms of each binomial
- **Last**: Multiply the last term of each binomial

Using FOIL, $(Ax + By)(Cx + Dy) = ACx^2 + ADxy + BCxy + BDy^2$.

> **Review Video: Multiplying Terms Using the Foil Method**
> Visit mometrix.com/academy and enter code: 854792

To **divide** polynomials, begin by arranging the terms of each polynomial in order of one variable. You may arrange in ascending or descending order, but be consistent with both polynomials. To get the first term of the quotient, divide the first term of the dividend by the first term of the divisor. Multiply the first term of the quotient by the entire divisor and subtract that product from the dividend. Repeat for the second and successive terms until you either get a remainder of zero or a remainder whose degree is less than the degree of the divisor. If the quotient has a remainder, write the answer as a mixed expression in the form: quotient $+ \frac{\text{remainder}}{\text{divisor}}$.

Rational expressions are fractions with polynomials in both the numerator and the denominator; the value of the polynomial in the denominator cannot be equal to zero. To *add or subtract* rational expressions, first find the common denominator, then rewrite each fraction as an equivalent fraction with the common denominator. Finally, add or subtract the numerators to get the numerator of the answer, and keep the common denominator as the denominator of the answer. When *multiplying* rational expressions factor each polynomial and cancel like factors (a factor which appears in both the numerator and the denominator). Then, multiply all remaining factors in the numerator to get the numerator of the product, and multiply the remaining factors in the denominator to get the denominator of the product. Remember – cancel entire factors, not individual terms. To *divide* rational expressions, take the reciprocal of the divisor (the rational expression you are dividing by) and multiply by the dividend.

> **Review Video: Simplifying Rational Polynomial Functions**
> Visit mometrix.com/academy and enter code: 351038

Below are patterns of some special products to remember: perfect trinomial squares, the difference between two squares, the sum and difference of two cubes, and perfect cubes.

- **Perfect Trinomial Squares**: $x^2 + 2xy + y^2 = (x + y)^2$ or $x^2 - 2xy + y^2 = (x - y)^2$
- **Difference Between Two Squares**: $x^2 - y^2 = (x + y)(x - y)$
- **Sum of Two Cubes**: $x^3 + y^3 = (x + y)(x^2 - xy + y^2)$
- Note: the second factor is NOT the same as a perfect trinomial square, so do not try to factor it further.
- **Difference Between Two Cubes**: $x^3 - y^3 = (x - y)(x^2 + xy + y^2)$
- Again, the second factor is NOT the same as a perfect trinomial square.
- **Perfect Cubes**: $x^3 + 3x^2y + 3xy^2 + y^3 = (x + y)^3$ and $x^3 - 3x^2y + 3xy^2 - y^3 = (x - y)^3$

In order to *factor* a polynomial, first check for a **common monomial factor**. When the greatest common monomial factor has been factored out, look for patterns of special products: differences of two squares, the sum or difference of two cubes for binomial factors, or perfect trinomial squares for trinomial factors. If the factor is a trinomial but not a perfect trinomial square, look for a factorable form, such as $x^2 + (a + b)x + ab = (x + a)(x + b)$ or $(ac)x^2 + (ad + bc)x + bd = (ax + b)(cx + d)$. For factors with four terms, look for groups to factor. Once you have found the factors, write the original polynomial as the product of all the factors. Make sure all of the polynomial factors are prime. Monomial factors may be *prime* or *composite*. Check your work by multiplying the factors to make sure you get the original polynomial.

Solving Quadratic Equations

The **quadratic formula** is used to solve quadratic equations when other methods are more difficult. To use the quadratic formula to solve a quadratic equation, begin by rewriting the equation in standard form $ax^2 + bx + c = 0$, where a, b, and c are *coefficients*. Once you have identified the values of the coefficients, substitute those values into the quadratic formula $x = \frac{-b \pm \sqrt{b^2 - 4ac}}{2a}$. Evaluate the equation and simplify the expression. Again, check each root by substituting into the original equation. In the quadratic formula, the portion of the formula under the radical ($b^2 - 4ac$) is called the **discriminant**. If the discriminant is zero, there is only one root: zero. If the discriminant is positive, there are two different real roots. If the discriminant is negative, there are no real roots.

> **Review Video: Using the Quadratic Formula**
> Visit mometrix.com/academy and enter code: 163102

To solve a quadratic equation by **factoring**, begin by rewriting the equation in standard form, if necessary. Factor the side with the variable then set each of the factors equal to zero and solve the resulting linear equations. Check your answers by *substituting* the roots you found into the original equation. If, when writing the equation in standard form, you have an equation in the form $x^2 + c = 0$ or $x^2 - c = 0$, set $x^2 = -c$ or $x^2 = c$ and take the square root of c. If c = 0, the only real root is zero. If c is positive, there are two real roots—the positive and negative square root values. If c is negative, there are no real roots because you cannot take the square root of a negative number.

> **Review Video: Factoring Quadratic Equations**
> Visit mometrix.com/academy and enter code: 336566

To solve a quadratic equation by **completing the square**, rewrite the equation so that all terms containing the variable are on the left side of the equal sign, and all the constants are on the right side of the equal sign. Make sure the coefficient of the squared term is 1. If there is a coefficient with the squared term, divide each term on both sides of the equal side by that number. Next, work with the coefficient of the single-variable term. Square half of this coefficient, and add that value to both sides. Now you can factor the left side (the side containing the variable) as the square of a binomial. $x^2 + 2ax + a^2 = C \Rightarrow (x + a)^2 = C$, where x is the variable, and a and C are constants. Take the square root of both sides and solve for the variable. Substitute the value of the variable in the original problem to check your work.

Other Important Concepts

Commonly in algebra and other upper-level fields of math you find yourself working with mathematical expressions that do not equal each other. The statement comparing such expressions with symbols such as < (less than) or > (greater than) is called an **inequality**. An example of an inequality is $7x > 5$. To solve for x, simply divide both sides by 7 and the solution is shown to be $x > \frac{5}{7}$. Graphs of the solution set of inequalities are represented on a number line. Open circles are used to show that an expression approaches a number but is never quite equal to that number.

Conditional inequalities are those with certain values for the variable that will make the condition true and other values for the variable where the condition will be false. **Absolute inequalities** can have any real number as the value for the variable to make the condition true, while there is no real number value for the variable that will make the condition false. Solving inequalities is done by following the same rules as for solving equations with the exception that when multiplying or dividing by a negative number the direction of the inequality sign must be flipped or reversed. **Double inequalities** are situations where two inequality statements apply to the same variable expression. An example of this is $-c < ax + b < c$.

A **weighted mean**, or weighted average, is a mean that uses "weighted" values. The formula is weighted mean $= \frac{w_1 x_1 + w_2 x_2 + w_3 x_3 \ldots + w_n x_n}{w_1 + w_2 + w_3 + \cdots + w_n}$. Weighted values, such as $w_1, w_2, w_3, \ldots w_n$ are assigned to each member of the set $x_1, x_2, x_3, \ldots x_n$. If calculating weighted mean, make sure a weight value for each member of the set is used.

A fraction that contains a fraction in the numerator, denominator, or both is called a **complex fraction**. These can be solved in a number of ways; with the simplest being by following the order of operations as stated earlier. For example,

$\frac{\left(\frac{4}{7}\right)}{\left(\frac{5}{8}\right)} = \frac{0.5714}{0.625} = 0.914$. Another way to solve this problem is to multiply the fraction in the numerator

by the reciprical of the fraction in the denominator. For example, $\frac{\left(\frac{4}{7}\right)}{\left(\frac{5}{8}\right)} = \frac{4}{7} \times \frac{8}{5} = \frac{32}{35} = 0.914$.

In order to solve a **radical equation**, begin by isolating the radical term on one side of the equation, and move all other terms to the other side of the equation. Look at the **index** of the radicand. Remember, if no number is given, the index is 2, meaning square root. Raise both sides of the equation to the power equal to the index of the radical. Solve the resulting equation as you would a normal polynomial equation. When you have found the roots, you must check them in the original problem to eliminate extraneous roots.

The **solution set** is the set of all solutions of an equation. Many equations will only have one value in their solution set. If there were more solutions then they would also be included in the solution set. When an equation has no true solutions, this is referred to as an **empty set**.

College-Level Math Test

Solving Systems of Equations

Systems of equations are a set of simultaneous equations that all use the same variables. A solution to a system of equations must be true for each equation in the system. **Consistent systems** are those with at least one solution. **Inconsistent systems** are systems of equations that have no solution.

To solve a system of linear equations by **substitution**, start with the easier equation and solve for one of the variables. Express this variable in terms of the other variable. Substitute this expression in the other equation, and solve for the other variable. The solution should be expressed in the form (x, y). Substitute the values into both of the original equations to check your answer. Consider the following problem.

Solve the system using substitution:

$$x + 6y = 15$$

$$3x - 12y = 18$$

Solving the first equation for x:

$$x = 15 - 6y$$

Substitute this value in place of x in the second equation, and solve for y:

$$3(15 - 6y) - 12y = 18$$

$$45 - 18y - 12y = 18$$

$$30y = 27$$

$$y = \frac{27}{30} = \frac{9}{10} = 0.9$$

Plug this value for y back into the first equation to solve for x:

$$x = 15 - 6(0.9) = 15 - 5.4 = 9.6$$

Check both equations if you have time:

$$9.6 + 6(0.9) = 9.6 + 5.4 = 15$$

$$3(9.6) - 12(0.9) = 28.8 - 10.8 = 18$$

Therefore, the solution is $(9.6, 0.9)$.

To solve a system of equations using **elimination**, begin by rewriting both equations in standard form $Ax + By = C$. Check to see if the coefficients of one pair of like variables add to zero. If not, multiply one or both of the equations by a non-zero number to make one set of like variables add to zero. Add the two equations to solve for one of the variables. Substitute this value into one of the

26

original equations to solve for the other variable. Check your work by substituting into the other equation. Next we will solve the same problem as above, but using the addition method.

Solve the system using elimination:

$$x + 6y = 15$$

$$3x - 12y = 18$$

If we multiply the first equation by 2, we can eliminate the y terms:

$$2x + 12y = 30$$

$$3x - 12y = 18$$

Add the equations together and solve for x:

$5x = 48$

$$x = \frac{48}{5} = 9.6$$

Plug the value for x back in to either of the original equations and solve for y:

$9.6 + 6y = 15$

$$y = \frac{15 - 9.6}{6} = 0.9$$

Check both equations if you have time:

$$9.6 + 6(0.9) = 9.6 + 5.4 = 15$$

$$3(9.6) - 12(0.9) = 28.8 - 10.8 = 18$$

Therefore, the solution is (9.6, 0.9).

Review Video: <u>Substitution and Elimination for Solving Linear Systems</u>
Visit mometrix.com/academy and enter code: 958611

Equations and Graphing

When algebraic functions and equations are shown graphically, they are usually shown on a **Cartesian coordinate plane**. The Cartesian coordinate plane consists of two number lines placed perpendicular to each other, and intersecting at the zero point, also known as the **origin**. The horizontal number line is known as the **x-axis**, with positive values to the right of the origin, and negative values to the left of the origin. The vertical number line is known as the **y-axis**, with positive values above the origin, and negative values below the origin. Any point on the plane can be identified by an ordered pair in the form (x,y), called **coordinates**. The x-value of the coordinate is called the **abscissa**, and the y-value of the coordinate is called the **ordinate**.

The two number lines divide the plane into four **quadrants**: I, II, III, and IV.

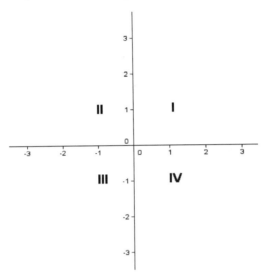

Before learning the different forms equations can be written in, it is important to understand some terminology. A ratio of the change in the vertical distance to the change in horizontal distance is called the **slope**. On a graph with two points, (x_1, y_1) and (x_2, y_2), the slope is represented by the formula $m = \frac{y_2 - y_1}{x_2 - x_1}$; $x_1 \neq x_2$. If the value of the slope is positive, the line slopes upward from left to right. If the value of the slope is negative, the line slopes downward from left to right. If the y-coordinates are the same for both points, the slope is 0 and the line is a **horizontal line**. If the x-coordinates are the same for both points, there is no slope and the line is a **vertical line**. Two or more lines that have equal slopes are **parallel lines**. **Perpendicular lines** have slopes that are negative reciprocals of each other, such as $\frac{a}{b}$ and $\frac{-b}{a}$.

As mentioned previously, equations can be written many ways. Below is a list of the many forms equations can take.

- **Standard form:** $Ax + By = C$; the slope is $\frac{-A}{B}$ and the y-intercept is $\frac{C}{B}$
- **Slope-intercept form:** $y = mx + b$, where m is the slope and b is the y-intercept
- **Point-slope form:** $y - y_1 = m(x - x_1)$, where m is the slope and (x_1, y_1) is a point on the line
- **Two-point form:** $\frac{y - y_1}{x - x_1} = \frac{y_2 - y_1}{x_2 - x_1}$, where (x_1, y_1) and (x_2, y_2) are two points on the given line
- **Intercept form:** $\frac{x}{x_1} + \frac{y}{y_1} = 1$, where $(x_1, 0)$ is the point at which a line intersects the x-axis, and $(0, y_1)$ is the point at which the same line intersects the y-axis

Equations can also be written as $ax + b = 0$, where $a \neq 0$. These are referred to as **one variable linear equations**. A solution to such an equation is called a **root**. In the case where we have the equation $5x + 10 = 0$, if we solve for x we get a solution of $x = -2$. In other words, the root of the equation is –2. This is found by first subtracting 10 from both sides, which gives $5x = -10$. Next, simply divide both sides by the coefficient of the variable, in this case 5, to get $x = -2$. This can be checked by plugging –2 back into the original equation :

$(5)(-2) + 10 = -10 + 10 = 0.$

CALCULATIONS USING POINTS

Sometimes you need to perform calculations using only points on a graph as input data. Using points, you can determine what the midpoint and distance are. If you know the equation for a line you can calculate the distance between the line and the point.

To find the **midpoint** of two points (x_1, y_1) and (x_2, y_2), average the x-coordinates to get the x-coordinate of the midpoint, and average the y-coordinates to get the y-coordinate of the midpoint. The formula is midpoint $= \left(\frac{x_1+x_2}{2}, \frac{y_1+y_2}{2}\right)$.

The **distance** between two points is the same as the length of the hypotenuse of a right triangle with the two given points as endpoints, and the two sides of the right triangle parallel to the x-axis and y-axis, respectively. The length of the segment parallel to the x-axis is the difference between the x-coordinates of the two points. The length of the segment parallel to the y-axis is the difference between the y-coordinates of the two points.

Use the **Pythagorean Theorem** $a^2 + b^2 = c^2$ or $c = \sqrt{a^2 + b^2}$ to find the distance. The formula is: distance $= \sqrt{(x_2 - x_1)^2 + (y_2 - y_1)^2}$.

When a line is in the format $Ax + By + C = 0$, where A, B, and C are coefficients, you can use a point (x_1, y_1) not on the line and apply the formula $d = \frac{|Ax_1 + By_1 + C|}{\sqrt{A^2 + B^2}}$ to find the distance between the line and the point (x_1, y_1).

> **Review Video: Distance & Midpoint for Points on the Coordinate Plane**
> Visit mometrix.com/academy and enter code: 973653

Functions

A function is an equation that has exactly one value of output variable (**dependent variable**) for each value of the input variable (**independent variable**). The set of all values for the input variable (here assumed to be x) is the domain of the function, and the set of all corresponding values of output variable (here assumed to be y) is the range of the function. When looking at a graph of an equation, the easiest way to determine if the equation is a function or not is to conduct the **vertical line test**. If a vertical line drawn through any value of x crosses the graph in more than one place, the equation is not a function.

In functions with the notation $f(x)$, the value substituted for x in the equation is called the **argument**. The **domain** is the set of all values for x in a function. Unless otherwise given, assume the domain is the set of real numbers that will yield real numbers for the range. This is the domain of definition.

The **graph** of a function is the set of all ordered pairs (x, y) that satisfy the equation of the function. The points that have zero as the value for y are called the **zeros** of the function. These are also the **x-intercepts**, because that is the point at which the graph crosses, or intercepts, the x-axis. The points that have zero as the value for x are the y-intercepts because that is where the graph crosses the y-axis.

Any time there are **vertical asymptotes** or holes in a graph, such that the complete graph cannot be drawn as one continuous line, a graph is said to have **discontinuities**. Examples would include the graphs of hyperbolas that are functions, and the function $f(x) = \tan x$.

MANIPULATION OF FUNCTIONS

Horizontal and **vertical shift** occur when values are added to or subtracted from the x or y values, respectively.

If a constant is added to the y portion of each point, the graph shifts **up**. If a constant is subtracted from the y portion of each point, the graph shifts **down**. This is represented by the expression $f(x) \pm k$, where k is a constant.

If a constant is added to the x portion of each point, the graph shifts **left**. If a constant is subtracted from the x portion of each point, the graph shifts **right**. This is represented by the expression $f(x \pm k)$, where k is a constant.

Stretch, compression, and reflection occur when different parts of a function are multiplied by different groups of constants. If the function as a whole is multiplied by a real number constant greater than 1 ($k \times f(x)$), the graph is **stretched vertically**. If k in the previous equation is greater than zero but less than 1, the graph is **compressed vertically**. If k is less than zero, the graph is **reflected about the x-axis**, in addition to being either stretched or compressed vertically if k is less than or greater than -1, respectively.

If instead, just the x-term is multiplied by a constant greater than 1 ($f(k \times x)$), the graph is **compressed horizontally**. If k in the previous equation is greater than zero but less than 1, the graph is **stretched horizontally**. If k is less than zero, the graph is **reflected about the y-axis**, in addition to being either stretched or compressed horizontally if k is greater than or less than -1, respectively.

CLASSIFICATION OF FUNCTIONS

There are many different ways to classify functions based on their structure or behavior. Listed here are a few common classifications.

Constant functions are given by the equation $y = b$ or $f(x) = b$, where b is a real number. There is no independent variable present in the equation, so the function has a constant value for all x. The graph of a constant function is a horizontal line of slope 0 that is positioned b units from the x-axis. If b is positive, the line is above the x-axis; if b is negative, the line is below the x-axis.

Identity functions are identified by the equation $y = x$ or $f(x) = x$, where every value of y is equal to its corresponding value of x. The only zero is the point $(0, 0)$. The graph is a diagonal line with slope 1.

In **linear functions**, the value of the function changes in direct proportion to x. The rate of change, represented by the slope on its graph, is constant throughout. The standard form of a linear equation is $ax + by = c$, where a, b, and c are real numbers. As a function, this equation is commonly written as $y = mx + b$ or $f(x) = mx + b$. This is known as the slope-intercept form, because the coefficients give the slope of the graphed function (m) and its y-intercept (b). Solve the equation $mx + b = 0$ for x to get $x = -\frac{b}{m}$, which is the only zero of the function. The domain and range are both the set of all real numbers.

A **polynomial function** is a function with multiple terms and multiple powers of x, such as

$$f(x) = a_n x^n + a_{n-1} x^{n-1} + a_{n-2} x^{n-2} + \cdots + a_1 x + a_0$$

where n is a non-negative integer that is the highest exponent in the polynomial, and $a_n \neq 0$. The domain of a polynomial function is the set of all real numbers. If the greatest exponent in the polynomial is even, the polynomial is said to be of even degree and the range is the set of real numbers that satisfy the function. If the greatest exponent in the polynomial is odd, the polynomial is said to be odd and the range, like the domain, is the set of all real numbers.

A **quadratic function** is a polynomial function that follows the equation pattern $y = ax^2 + bx + c$, or $f(x) = ax^2 + bx + c$, where a, b, and c are real numbers and $a \neq 0$. The domain of a quadratic function is the set of all real numbers. The range is also real numbers, but only those in the subset of the domain that satisfy the equation. To determine the number of roots of a quadratic equation, solve the expression $b^2 - 4ac$. If this value is positive, there are two unique real roots. If this value equals zero, there is one real root, which is a double root. If this value is less than zero, there are no real roots. The root(s) of any quadratic function can be found by plugging the values of a, b, and c into the **quadratic formula**:

$$x = \frac{-b \pm \sqrt{b^2 - 4ac}}{2a}$$

If the expression $b^2 - 4ac$ is negative, you will instead find complex roots.

A quadratic function has a parabola for its graph. In the equation $f(x) = ax^2 + bx + c$, if a is positive, the parabola will open upward. If a is negative, the parabola will open downward. The **axis of symmetry** is a vertical line that passes through the vertex.

To determine whether or not the parabola will intersect the x-axis, check the number of real roots. An equation with two real roots will cross the x-axis twice. An equation with one real root will have its vertex on the x-axis. An equation with no real roots will not contact the x-axis.

A **rational function** is a function that can be constructed as a ratio of two polynomial expressions: $f(x) = \frac{p(x)}{q(x)}$, where $p(x)$ and $q(x)$ are both polynomial expressions and $q(x) \neq 0$. The **domain** is the set of all real numbers, except any values for which $q(x) = 0$. The **range** is the set of real numbers that satisfies the function when the domain is applied. When you graph a rational function, you will have vertical asymptotes wherever $q(x) = 0$. If the polynomial in the numerator is of lesser degree than the polynomial in the denominator, the x-axis will also be a horizontal asymptote. If the numerator and denominator have equal degrees, there will be a horizontal asymptote not on the x-axis. If the degree of the numerator is exactly one greater than the degree of the denominator, the graph will have an oblique, or diagonal, asymptote. The asymptote will be along the line $y = \frac{p_n}{q_{n-1}} x + \frac{p_{n-1}}{q_{n-1}}$, where p_n and q_{n-1} are the coefficients of the highest degree terms in their respective polynomials.

A **square root function** is a function that contains a radical and is in the format $f(x) = \sqrt{ax + b}$. The domain is the set of all real numbers that yields a positive radicand or a radicand equal to zero. Because square root values are assumed to be positive unless otherwise identified, the range is all real numbers from zero to infinity. To find the zero of a square root function, set the radicand equal to zero and solve for x. The graph of a square root function is always to the right of the zero and always above the x-axis.

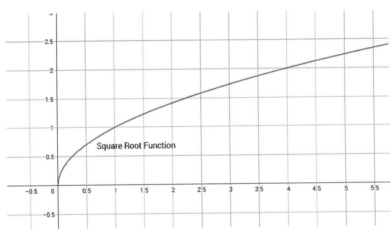

An **absolute value function** is in the format $f(x) = |ax + b|$. Like other functions, the domain is the set of all real numbers. However, because absolute value indicates positive numbers, the range is limited to positive real numbers. To find the zero of an absolute value function, set the portion inside the absolute value sign equal to zero and solve for x. An absolute value function is also known as a piecewise function because it must be solved in pieces – one for if the value inside the absolute value sign is positive, and one for if the value is negative. The function can be expressed as

$$f(x) = \begin{cases} ax + b \text{ if } ax + b \geq 0 \\ -(ax + b) \text{ if } ax + b < 0 \end{cases}$$

This will allow for an accurate statement of the range.

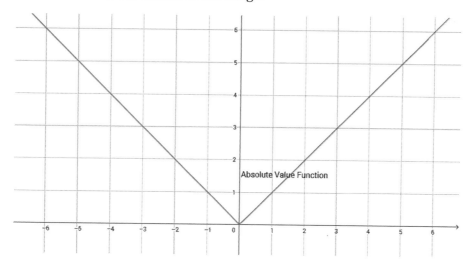

Absolute Value Function

Exponential functions are equations that have the format $y = b^x$, where base $b > 0$ and $b \neq 1$. The exponential function can also be written $f(x) = b^x$.

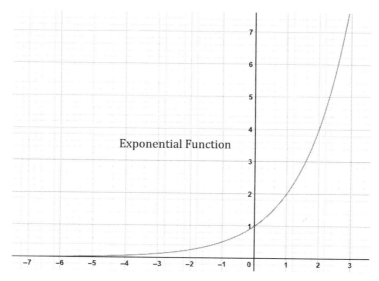

Exponential Function

Logarithmic functions are equations that have the format $y = \log_b x$ or $f(x) = \log_b x$. The base b may be any number except one; however, the most common bases for logarithms are base 10 and base e. The log base e is known the **natural logarithm**, or ln, expressed by the function $f(x) = \ln x$. Any logarithm that does not have an assigned value of b is assumed to be base 10: $\log x = \log_{10} x$. Exponential functions and logarithmic functions are related in that one is the inverse of the other. If

33

$f(x) = b^x$, then $f^{-1}(x) = \log_b x$. This can perhaps be expressed more clearly by the two equations: $y = b^x$ and $x = \log_b y$.

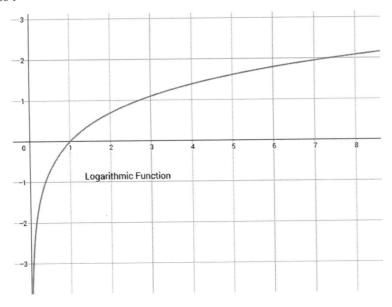

The following properties apply to logarithmic expressions:

$$\log_b 1 = 0$$

$$\log_b b = 1$$

$$\log_b b^p = p$$

$$\log_b MN = \log_b M + \log_b N$$

$$\log_b \frac{M}{N} = \log_b M - \log_b N$$

$$\log_b M^p = p \log_b M$$

In a **one-to-one function**, each value of x has exactly one value for y (this is the definition of a function) *and* each value of y has exactly one value for x. While the vertical line test will determine if a graph is that of a function, the horizontal line test will determine if a function is a one-to-one function. If a horizontal line drawn at any value of y intersects the graph in more than one place, the graph is not that of a one-to-one function. Do not make the mistake of using the horizontal line test exclusively in determining if a graph is that of a one-to-one function. A one-to-one function must pass both the vertical line test and the horizontal line test. One-to-one functions are also **invertible functions**.

A **monotone function** is a function whose graph either constantly increases or constantly decreases. Examples include the functions $f(x) = x$, $f(x) = -x$, or $f(x) = x^3$.

An **even function** has a graph that is symmetric with respect to the y-axis and satisfies the equation $f(x) = f(-x)$. Examples include the functions $f(x) = x^2$ and $f(x) = ax^n$, where a is any real number and n is a positive even integer.

An **odd function** has a graph that is symmetric with respect to the origin and satisfies the equation $f(x) = -f(-x)$. Examples include the functions $f(x) = x^3$ and $f(x) = ax^n$, where a is any real number and n is a positive odd integer.

Algebraic functions are those that exclusively use polynomials and roots. These would include polynomial functions, rational functions, square root functions, and all combinations of these functions, such as polynomials as the radicand. These combinations may be joined by addition, subtraction, multiplication, or division, but may not include variables as exponents.

Transcendental functions are all functions that are non-algebraic. Any function that includes logarithms, trigonometric functions, variables as exponents, or any combination that includes any of these is not algebraic in nature, even if the function includes polynomials or roots.

RELATED CONCEPTS

According to the **Fundamental Theorem of Algebra**, every non-constant, single variable polynomial has exactly as many roots as the polynomial's *highest exponent*. For example, if x^4 is the largest exponent of a term, the polynomial will have exactly 4 roots. However, some of these roots may have multiplicity or be non-real numbers. For instance, in the polynomial function $f(x) = x^4 - 4x + 3$, the only real roots are 1 and -1. The root 1 has multiplicity of 2 and there is one non-real root $(-1 - \sqrt{2}i)$.

The **Remainder Theorem** is useful for determining the remainder when a polynomial is divided by a binomial. The Remainder Theorem states that if a polynomial function $f(x)$ is divided by a binomial $x - a$, where a is a real number, the remainder of the division will be the value of $f(a)$. If $f(a) = 0$, then a is a root of the polynomial.

The **Factor Theorem** is related to the Remainder Theorem and states that if $f(a) = 0$ then $(x - a)$ is a factor of the function.

According to the **Rational Root Theorem,** any rational root of a polynomial function $f(x) = a_n x^n + a_{n-1} x^{n-1} + \cdots + a_1 x + a_0$ with integer coefficients will, when reduced to its lowest terms, be a positive or negative fraction such that the numerator is a factor of a_0 and the denominator is a factor of a_n. For instance, if the polynomial function $f(x) = x^3 + 3x^2 - 4$ has any rational roots, the numerators of those roots can only be factors of 4 (1, 2, 4), and the denominators can only be factors of 1 (1). The function in this example has roots of 1 (or $\frac{1}{1}$) and -2 (or $-\frac{2}{1}$).

Variables that vary **directly** are those that either both increase at the same rate or both decrease at the same rate. For example, in the functions $f(x) = kx$ or $f(x) = kx^n$, where k and n are positive, the value of $f(x)$ increases as the value of x increases and decreases as the value of x decreases.

Variables that vary **inversely** are those where one increases while the other decreases. For example, in the functions $f(x) = \frac{k}{x}$ or $f(x) = \frac{k}{x^n}$ where k is a positive constant, the value of y increases as the value of x decreases, and the value of y decreases as the value of x increases.

In both cases, k is the **constant** of variation.

APPLYING THE BASIC OPERATIONS TO FUNCTIONS

For each of the basic functions, we will use these functions as examples: $f(x) = x^2$ and $g(x) = x$.

To find the **sum** of two functions f and g, assuming the domains are compatible, simply add the two functions together:

$$(f + g)(x) = f(x) + g(x) = x^2 + x$$

To find the **difference** of two functions f and g, assuming the domains are compatible, simply subtract the second function from the first:

$$(f - g)(x) = f(x) - g(x) = x^2 - x$$

To find the **product** of two functions f and g, assuming the domains are compatible, multiply the two functions together:

$$(f \cdot g)(x) = f(x) \cdot g(x) = x^2 \cdot x = x^3$$

To find the **quotient** of two functions f and g, assuming the domains are compatible, divide the first function by the second:

$$\frac{f}{g}(x) = \frac{f(x)}{g(x)} = \frac{x^2}{x} = x \; ; x \neq 0$$

The example given in each case is fairly simple, but on a given problem, if you are looking only for the value of the sum, difference, product or quotient of two functions at a particular x-value, it may be simpler to solve the functions individually and then perform the given operation using those values.

The **composite** of two functions f and g, written as $(f \circ g)(x)$ simply means that the output of the second function is used as the input of the first. This can also be written as $f(g(x))$. In general, this can be solved by substituting $g(x)$ for all instances of x in $f(x)$ and simplifying. Using the example functions $f(x) = x^2 - x + 2$ and $g(x) = x + 1$, we can find that $(f \circ g)(x)$ or $f(g(x))$ is equal to $f(x + 1) = (x + 1)^2 - (x + 1) + 2$, which simplifies to $x^2 + x + 2$.

It is important to note that $(f \circ g)(x)$ is not necessarily the same as $(g \circ f)(x)$. The process is not *commutative* like addition or multiplication expressions. If $(f \circ g)(x)$ does equal $(g \circ f)(x)$, the two functions are **inverses** of each other.

Trigonometry

The three basic trigonometric functions are sine, cosine, and tangent.

SINE

The sine (sin) function has a period of 360° or 2π radians. This means that its graph makes one complete cycle every 360° or 2π. Because sin 0 = 0, the graph of $y = \sin x$ begins at the **origin**, with the x-axis representing the angle measure, and the y-axis representing the sine of the angle. The graph of the sine function is a smooth curve that begins at the origin, peaks at the point $\left(\frac{\pi}{2}, 1\right)$, crosses the x-axis at $(\pi, 0)$, has its lowest point at $\left(\frac{3\pi}{2}, -1\right)$, and returns to the x-axis to complete one cycle at $(2\pi, 0)$.

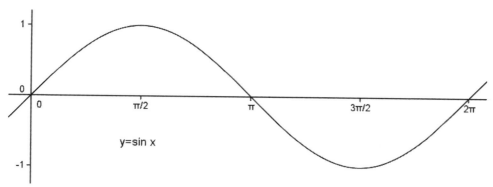

COSINE

The cosine (cos) function also has a period of 360° or 2π radians, which means that its graph also makes one complete cycle every 360° or 2π. Because cos 0° = 1, the graph of $y = \cos x$ begins at the point $(0, 1)$, with the x-axis representing the angle measure, and the y-axis representing the cosine of the angle.

The graph of the cosine function is a smooth curve that begins at the point $(0, 1)$, crosses the x-axis at the point $\left(\frac{\pi}{2}, 0\right)$, has its lowest point at $(\pi, -1)$, crosses the x-axis again at the point $\left(\frac{3\pi}{2}, 0\right)$, and returns to a peak at the point $(2\pi, 1)$ to complete one cycle.

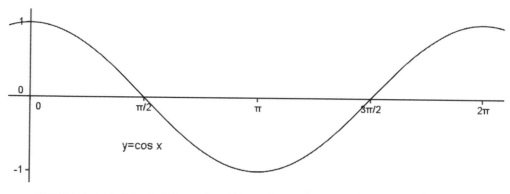

Review Video: Cosine
Visit mometrix.com/academy and enter code: 361120

TANGENT

The tangent (tan) function has a period of 180° or π radians, which means that its graph makes one complete cycle every 180° or π radians. The x-axis represents the angle measure, and the y-axis represents the tangent of the angle.

The graph of the tangent function is a series of smooth curves that cross the x-axis at every 180° or π radians and have an **asymptote** every $k \cdot 90°$ or $\frac{k\pi}{2}$ radians, where k is an odd integer. This can be explained by the fact that the tangent is calculated by dividing the sine by the cosine, since the cosine equals zero at those asymptote points.

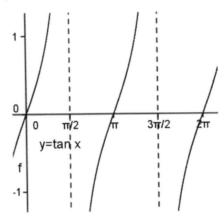

DEFINED AND RECIPROCAL FUNCTIONS

The tangent function is defined as the **ratio** of the sine to the cosine:

Tangent (tan):

$$\tan x = \frac{\sin x}{\cos x}$$

To take the **reciprocal** of a number means to place that number as the denominator of a fraction with a numerator of 1. The reciprocal functions are thus defined quite simply.

Cosecant (csc):

$$\csc x = \frac{1}{\sin x}$$

Secant (sec):

$$\sec x = \frac{1}{\cos x}$$

Cotangent (cot):

$$\cot x = \frac{1}{\tan x}$$

It is important to know these reciprocal functions, but they are not as commonly used as the three basic functions.

INVERSE FUNCTIONS

Each of the trigonometric functions accepts an angular measure, either degrees or radians, and gives a numerical value as the output. The inverse functions do the opposite; they accept a numerical value and give an angular measure as the output. The **inverse sine**, or arcsine, commonly written as either $\sin^{-1} x$ or arcsin x, gives the angle whose sine is x.

Similarly:

The **inverse of cos x** is written as $\cos^{-1} x$ or arccos x and means the angle whose cosine is x.

The **inverse of tan x** is written as $\tan^{-1} x$ or arctan x and means the angle whose tangent is x.

The **inverse of csc x** is written as $\csc^{-1} x$ or arccsc x and means the angle whose cosecant is x.

The **inverse of sec x** is written as $\sec^{-1} x$ or arcsec x and means the angle whose secant is x.

The **inverse of cot x** is written as $\cot^{-1} x$ or arccot x and means the angle whose cotangent is x.

SOLUTIONS TO TRIGONOMETRIC EQUATIONS

Trigonometric and algebraic equations are solved following the same rules, but while algebraic expressions have one unique solution, trigonometric equations could have **multiple solutions**, and you must find them all. When solving for an angle with a known trigonometric value, you must consider the sign and include all angles with that value.

Your calculator will probably only give one value as an answer, typically in the following ranges:

For the inverse sine function, $\left[-\frac{\pi}{2}, \frac{\pi}{2}\right]$ or $[-90°, 90°]$

For the inverse cosine function, $[0, \pi]$ or $[0°, 180°]$

For the inverse tangent function, $\left[-\frac{\pi}{2}, \frac{\pi}{2}\right]$ or $[-90°, 90°]$

It is important to determine if there is another angle in a **different quadrant** that also satisfies the problem. To do this, find the other quadrant(s) with the same sign for that trigonometric function and find the angle that has the same reference angle. Then check whether this angle is also a solution.

In the first quadrant, all six trigonometric functions are **positive** (sin, cos, tan, csc, sec, cot). In the second quadrant, sin and csc are positive. In the third quadrant, tan and cot are positive. In the fourth quadrant, cos and sec are positive.

If you remember the phrase, "ALL Students Take Classes," you will be able to remember the sign of each trigonometric function in each quadrant. **ALL** represents all the signs in the first quadrant. The "**S**" in "Students" represents the sine function and its reciprocal in the second quadrant. The "**T**" in

"Take" represents the tangent function and its reciprocal in the third quadrant. The "**C**" in "Classes" represents the cosine function and its reciprocal.

TRIGONOMETRIC IDENTITIES

SUM AND DIFFERENCE

To find the sine, cosine, or tangent of the **sum** or **difference** of two angles, use one of the following formulas:

$$\sin(\alpha \pm \beta) = \sin\alpha\cos\beta \pm \cos\alpha\sin\beta$$

$$\cos(\alpha \pm \beta) = \cos\alpha\cos\beta \mp \sin\alpha\sin\beta$$

$$\tan(\alpha \pm \beta) = \frac{\tan\alpha \pm \tan\beta}{1 \mp \tan\alpha\tan\beta}$$

where α and β are two angles with known sine, cosine, or tangent values as needed.

HALF ANGLE

To find the sine or cosine of **half** of a known angle, use the following formulas:

$$\sin\frac{\theta}{2} = \pm\sqrt{\frac{1-\cos\theta}{2}}$$

$$\cos\frac{\theta}{2} = \pm\sqrt{\frac{1+\cos\theta}{2}}$$

where θ is an angle with a known exact cosine value.

To determine the **sine** of the answer, you must notice the quadrant the given angle is in and apply the correct sign for the trigonometric function you are using. If you need to find the exact sine or cosine of an angle that you do not know, such as sine 22.5°, you can rewrite the given angle as a half angle, such as sine $\frac{45°}{2}$, and use the formula above.

To find the tangent or cotangent of **half** of a known angle, use the following formulas:

$$\tan\frac{\theta}{2} = \frac{\sin\theta}{1+\cos\theta}$$

$$\cot\frac{\theta}{2} = \frac{\sin\theta}{1-\cos\theta}$$

where θ is an angle with known exact sine and cosine values.

These formulas will work for finding the tangent or cotangent of half of any angle unless the cosine of θ happens to make the denominator of the identity equal to 0.

DOUBLE ANGLE

In each case, use one of the **Double Angle Formulas**.

To find the sine or cosine of twice a known angle, use one of the following formulas:

$$\sin(2\theta) = 2\sin\theta\cos\theta$$

$$\cos(2\theta) = \cos^2\theta - \sin^2\theta \text{ or}$$

$$\cos(2\theta) = 2\cos^2\theta - 1 \text{ or}$$

$$\cos(2\theta) = 1 - 2\sin^2\theta$$

To find the tangent or cotangent of twice a known angle, use the formulas:

$$\tan(2\theta) = \frac{2\tan\theta}{1 - \tan^2\theta}$$

$$\cot(2\theta) = \frac{\cot\theta - \tan\theta}{2}$$

In each case, θ is an angle with known exact sine, cosine, tangent, and cotangent values.

PRODUCTS

To find the **product** of the sines and cosines of two different angles, use one of the following formulas:

$$\sin\alpha\sin\beta = \frac{1}{2}[\cos(\alpha - \beta) - \cos(\alpha + \beta)]$$

$$\cos\alpha\cos\beta = \frac{1}{2}[\cos(\alpha + \beta) + \cos(\alpha - \beta)]$$

$$\sin\alpha\cos\beta = \frac{1}{2}[\sin(\alpha + \beta) + \sin(\alpha - \beta)]$$

$$\cos\alpha\sin\beta = \frac{1}{2}[\sin(\alpha + \beta) - \sin(\alpha - \beta)]$$

where α and β are two unique angles.

COMPLEMENTARY

The trigonometric cofunction identities use the trigonometric relationships of **complementary angles** (angles whose sum is 90°). These are:

$$\cos x = \sin(90° - x)$$

$$\csc x = \sec(90° - x)$$

$$\cot x = \tan(90° - x)$$

PYTHAGOREAN THEOREM

The Pythagorean Theorem states that $a^2 + b^2 = c^2$ for all right triangles. The **trigonometric identity** that derives from this principle is stated in this way:

$$\sin^2\theta + \cos^2\theta = 1$$

Dividing each term by either $\sin^2\theta$ or $\cos^2\theta$ yields two other identities, respectively:

$$1 + \cot^2\theta = \csc^2\theta$$

$$\tan^2\theta + 1 = \sec^2\theta$$

> **Review Video: Pythagorean Theorem**
> Visit mometrix.com/academy and enter code: 906576

UNIT CIRCLE

A unit circle is a circle with a **radius** of 1 that has its **center** at the origin. The equation of the unit circle is $x^2 + y^2 = 1$. Notice that this is an abbreviated version of the standard equation of a circle. Because the center is the point $(0, 0)$, the values of h and k in the general equation are equal to zero and the equation simplifies to this form.

> **Review Video: Unit Circles and Standard Position**
> Visit mometrix.com/academy and enter code: 333922

Standard Position: The position of an angle of measure θ whose vertex is at the origin, the initial side crosses the unit circle at the point $(1, 0)$, and the terminal side crosses the unit circle at some other point (a, b). In the standard position, $\sin\theta = b$, $\cos\theta = a$, and $\tan\theta = \frac{b}{a}$.

Rectangular coordinates are those that lie on the square grids of the Cartesian plane. They should be quite familiar to you. The **polar coordinate system** is based on a circular graph, rather than the square grid of the Cartesian system. Points in the polar coordinate system are in the format (r, θ), where r is the distance from the origin (think radius of the circle) and θ is the smallest positive angle (moving counterclockwise around the circle) made with the positive horizontal axis.

To **convert** a point from rectangular (x, y) format to polar (r, θ) format, use the formula (x, y) to $(r, \theta) \Rightarrow r = \sqrt{x^2 + y^2}; \theta = \arctan\frac{y}{x}$ when $x \neq 0$

If x is positive, use the positive square root value for r. If x is negative, use the negative square root value for r.

If x = 0, use the following rules:

If x = 0 and y = 0, then $\theta = 0$

If x = 0 and y > 0, then $\theta = \frac{\pi}{2}$

If x = 0 and y < 0, then $\theta = \frac{3\pi}{2}$

To **convert** a point from polar (r, θ) format to rectangular (x, y) format, use the formula (r, θ) to $(x, y) \Rightarrow x = r\cos\theta; y = r\sin\theta$

TABLE OF COMMONLY ENCOUNTERED ANGLES

$0° = 0$ radians, $30° = \frac{\pi}{6}$ radians, $45° = \frac{\pi}{4}$ radians, $60° = \frac{\pi}{3}$ radians, and $90° = \frac{\pi}{2}$ radians

$\sin 0° = 0$	$\cos 0° = 1$	$\tan 0° = 0$
$\sin 30° = \frac{1}{2}$	$\cos 30° = \frac{\sqrt{3}}{2}$	$\tan 30° = \frac{\sqrt{3}}{3}$
$\sin 45° = \frac{\sqrt{2}}{2}$	$\cos 45° = \frac{\sqrt{2}}{2}$	$\tan 45° = 1$
$\sin 60° = \frac{\sqrt{3}}{2}$	$\cos 60° = \frac{1}{2}$	$\tan 60° = \sqrt{3}$
$\sin 90° = 1$	$\cos 90° = 0$	$\tan 90° =$ undefined
$\csc 0° =$ undefined	$\sec 0° = 1$	$\cot 0° =$ undefined
$\csc 30° = 2$	$\sec 30° = \frac{2\sqrt{3}}{3}$	$\cot 30° = \sqrt{3}$
$\csc 45° = \sqrt{2}$	$\sec 45° = \sqrt{2}$	$\cot 45° = 1$
$\csc 60° = \frac{2\sqrt{3}}{3}$	$\sec 60° = 2$	$\cot 60° = \frac{\sqrt{3}}{3}$
$\csc 90° = 1$	$\sec 90° =$ undefined	$\cot 90° = 0$

The values in the upper half of this table are values you should have **memorized** or be able to find quickly.

Sequences and Series

A sequence is a set of numbers that continues on in a define pattern. The function that defines a sequence has a domain composed of the set of positive integers. Each member of the sequence is an **element**, or individual term. Each element is identified by the notation a_n, where a is the term of the sequence, and n is the integer identifying which term in the sequence a is. There are two different ways to represent a sequence that contains the element a_n.

The first is the **simple notation** $\{a_n\}$. The **expanded notation** of a sequence is $a_1, a_2, a_3, \ldots a_n, \ldots$. Notice that the expanded form does not end with the nth term. There is no indication that the nth term is the last term in the sequence, only that the nth term is an element of the sequence.

Some sequences will have a **limit**, or a value the sequence approaches or sometimes even reaches but never passes. A sequence that has a limit is known as a **convergent sequence** because all the values of the sequence seemingly converge at that point. Sequences that do not converge at a particular limit are **divergent sequences**. The easiest way to determine whether a sequence converges or diverges is to find the limit of the sequence. If the limit is a *real number*, the sequence is a convergent sequence. If the limit is *infinity*, the sequence is a divergent sequence. Remember the following rules for finding limits:

$$\lim_{n \to \infty} k = k \text{ for all real numbers } k$$

$$\lim_{n \to \infty} \frac{1}{n} = 0$$

$$\lim_{n \to \infty} n = \infty$$

$$\lim_{n \to \infty} \frac{k}{n^p} = 0 \text{ for all real numbers } k \text{ and positive rational numbers } p.$$

The limit of the **sums** of two sequences is equal to the sum of the limits of the two sequences:
$$\lim_{n \to \infty} (a_n + b_n) = \lim_{n \to \infty} a_n + \lim_{n \to \infty} b_n.$$

The limit of the **difference** between two sequences is equal to the difference between the limits of the two sequences:

$$\lim_{n \to \infty} (a_n - b_n) = \lim_{n \to \infty} a_n - \lim_{n \to \infty} b_n.$$

The limit of the **product** of two sequences is equal to the product of the limits of the two sequences:
$$\lim_{n \to \infty} (a_n \cdot b_n) = \lim_{n \to \infty} a_n \cdot \lim_{n \to \infty} b_n.$$

The limit of the **quotient** of two sequences is equal to the quotient of the limits of the two sequences, with some exceptions: $\lim_{n \to \infty} \left(\frac{a_n}{b_n} \right) = \frac{\lim_{n \to \infty} a_n}{\lim_{n \to \infty} b_n}$. In the quotient formula, it is important to consider that $b_n \neq 0$ and $\lim_{n \to \infty} b_n \neq 0$.

The limit of a sequence multiplied by a **scalar** is equal to the scalar multiplied by the limit of the sequence: $\lim_{n \to \infty} k a_n = k \lim_{n \to \infty} a_n$, where k is any real number.

A **monotonic sequence** is a sequence that is either nonincreasing or nondecreasing. The term *nonincreasing* is used to describe a sequence whose terms either get progressively smaller in value or remain the same. The term *nondecreasing* is used to describe a sequence whose terms either get progressively larger in value or remain the same. A nonincreasing sequence is bounded above. This means that all elements of the sequence must be less than a given real number. A nondecreasing sequence is bounded below. This means that all elements of the sequence must be greater than a given real number.

Whenever one element of a sequence is defined in terms of a previous element or elements of the sequence, the sequence is a **recursive sequence**. For example, given the recursive definition $a_1 = 0; a_2 = 1; a_n = a_{n-1} + a_{n-2}$ for all $n \geq 2$, you get the sequence 0, 1, 1, 2, 3, 5, 8, ... This particular sequence is known as the *Fibonacci sequence*, and is defined as the numbers zero and one, and a continuing sequence of numbers, with each number in the sequence equal to the sum of the two previous numbers. It is important to note that the Fibonacci sequence can also be defined as the first two terms being equal to one, with the remaining terms equal to the sum of the previous two terms. Both definitions are considered correct in mathematics. Make sure you know which definition you are working with when dealing with Fibonacci numbers.

Sometimes one term of a sequence with a recursive definition can be found without knowing the previous terms of the sequence. This case is known as a **closed-form expression** for a recursive definition. In this case, an alternate formula will apply to the sequence to generate the same sequence of numbers. However, not all sequences based on recursive definitions will have a closed-form expression. Some sequences will require the use of the recursive definition.

For example, the Fibonacci sequence has a closed-form expression given by the formula $a_n = \frac{\phi^n - \left(\frac{-1}{\phi}\right)^n}{\sqrt{5}}$, where φ is the golden ratio, which is equal to $\frac{1+\sqrt{5}}{2}$.

In this case, $a_0 = 0$ and $a_1 = 1$, so you know which definition of the Fibonacci sequence you have.

An **arithmetic sequence**, or arithmetic progression, is a special kind of sequence in which each term has a specific quantity, called the common difference, that is added to the previous term. The common difference may be positive or negative. The general form of an arithmetic sequence containing n terms is $a_1, a_1 + d, a_1 + 2d, ..., a_1 + (n-1)d$, where d is the common difference. The formula for the general term of an arithmetic sequence is $a_n = a_1 + (n-1)d$, where a_n is the term you are looking for and d is the common difference. To find the sum of the first n terms of an arithmetic sequence, use the formula $s_n = \frac{n}{2}(a_1 + a_n)$.

Review Video: Arithmetic Sequence
Visit mometrix.com/academy and enter code: 676885

A **geometric sequence**, or geometric progression, is a special kind of sequence in which each term has a specific quantity, called the common ratio, multiplied by the previous term. The common ratio may be positive or negative. The general form of a geometric sequence containing n terms is $a_1, a_1 r, a_1 r^2, ..., a_1 r^{n-1}$, where r is the common ratio. The formula for the general term of a geometric sequence is $a_n = a_1 r^{n-1}$, where a_n is the term you are looking for and r is the common ratio. To find the sum of the first n terms of a geometric sequence, use the formula $s_n = \frac{a_1(1-r^n)}{1-r}$.

Any function with the set of all **natural** numbers as the domain is also called a sequence. An element of a sequence is denoted by the symbol a_n, which represents the nth element of sequence a. Sequences may be arithmetic or geometric, and may be defined by a recursive definition, closed-form expression or both. Arithmetic and geometric sequences both have recursive definitions based on the first term of the sequence, as well as both having formulas to find the sum of the first n terms in the sequence, assuming you know what the first term is. The sum of all the terms in a sequence is called a **series**.

An **infinite series**, also referred to as just a series, is a series of partial sums of a defined sequence. Each infinite sequence represents an infinite series according to the equation $\sum_{n=1}^{\infty} a_n = a_1 + a_2 + a_3 + \cdots + a_n + \cdots$. This notation can be shortened to $\sum_{n=1}^{\infty} a_n$ or $\sum a_n$. Every series is a sequence of *partial sums*, where the first partial sum is equal to the first element of the series, the second partial sum is equal to the sum of the first two elements of the series, and the nth partial sum is equal to the sum of the first n elements of the series.

Every infinite sequence of partial sums either converges or diverges. Like the test for convergence in a sequence, finding the limit of the sequence of partial sums will indicate whether it is a converging series or a diverging series. If there exists a real number S such that $\lim_{n \to \infty} S_n = S$, where S_n is the sequence of partial sums, then the series **converges**. If the limit equals infinity, then the series **diverges**. If $\lim_{n \to \infty} S_n = S$ and S is a real number, then S is also the *convergence value* of the series.

To find the sum as n approaches infinity for the sum of two convergent series, find the sum as n approaches infinity for each individual series and **add** the results.

$$\sum_{n=1}^{\infty} (a_n + b_n) = \sum_{n=1}^{\infty} a_n + \sum_{n=1}^{\infty} b_n$$

To find the sum as n approaches infinity for the difference between two convergent series, find the sum as n approaches infinity for each individual series and **subtract** the results.

$$\sum_{n=1}^{\infty} (a_n - b_n) = \sum_{n=1}^{\infty} a_n - \sum_{n=1}^{\infty} b_n$$

To find the sum as n approaches infinity for the product of a scalar and a convergent series, find the sum as n approaches infinity for the series and **multiply** the result by the **scalar**.

$$\sum_{n=1}^{\infty} ka_n = k \sum_{n=1}^{\infty} a_n$$

A **geometric series** is an infinite series in which each term is multiplied by a constant real number r, called the **ratio**. This is represented by the equation

$$\sum_{n=1}^{\infty} ar^{n-1} = a_1 + a_2 r + a_3 r^2 + \cdots + a_n r^{n-1} + \cdots$$

If the absolute value of r is greater than or equal to one, then the geometric series is a **diverging series**. If the absolute value of r is less than one but greater than zero, the geometric series is a **converging series**. To find the sum of a converging geometric series, use the formula

$$\sum_{n=1}^{\infty} ar^{n-1} = \frac{a}{1-r}, \text{where } 0 < |r| < 1$$

46

The **n^{th} term test for divergence** involves taking the limit of the nth term of a sequence and determining whether or not the limit is equal to zero. If the limit of the nth term is not equal to zero, then the series is a diverging series. This test only works to prove divergence, however. If the nth term is equal to zero, the test is inconclusive.

Reading Comprehension Test

The Purpose of a Passage

Usually, identifying the **purpose** of an author is easier than identifying his or her position. In most cases, the author has no interest in hiding his or her purpose. A text that is meant to **entertain**, for instance, should be written to please the reader. Most narratives, or stories, are written to entertain, though they may also inform or persuade. **Informative texts** are easy to identify, while the most difficult purpose of a text to identify is **persuasion** because the author has an interest in making this purpose hard to detect. When a reader discovers that the author is trying to persuade, he or she should be skeptical of the argument. For this reason, persuasive texts often try to establish an entertaining tone and hope to amuse the reader into agreement. On the other hand, an informative tone may be implemented to create an appearance of authority and objectivity.

> **Review Video: Purpose**
> Visit mometrix.com/academy and enter code: 511819

An author's purpose is evident often in the **organization** of the text (e.g., section headings in bold font points to an informative text). However, you may not have such organization available to you in your exam. Instead, if the author makes his or her main idea clear from the beginning, then the likely purpose of the text is to **inform**. If the author begins by making a claim and provides various arguments to support that claim, then the purpose is probably to **persuade**. If the author tells a story or seems to want the attention of the reader more than to push a particular point or deliver information, then his or her purpose is most likely to **entertain**. As a reader, you must judge authors on how well they accomplish their purpose. In other words, you need to consider the type of passage (e.g., technical, persuasive, etc.) that the author has written and if the author has followed the requirements of the passage type.

An **informative text** is written to educate and enlighten readers. Informative texts are almost always nonfiction and are rarely structured as a story. The intention of an informative text is to deliver information in the most comprehensible way. So, look for the structure of the text to be very *clear*. In an informative text, the **thesis statement** (i.e., a stance or assertion on the topic of a text that is supported by evidence) is one or two sentences that normally appears at end of the first paragraph. The author may use some colorful language, but he or she is likely to put more emphasis on clarity and precision. Informative essays do not typically appeal to the emotions. They often contain facts and figures and rarely include the opinion of the author; however, readers should remain aware of the possibility for a bias as those facts are presented. Sometimes a persuasive essay can resemble an informative essay, especially if the author maintains an even tone and presents his or her views as if they were established fact.

> **Review Video: Informative Text**
> Visit mometrix.com/academy and enter code: 924964

In a sense, almost all writing is descriptive, insofar as an author seeks to describe events, ideas, or people to the reader. Some texts, however, are primarily concerned with **description**. A descriptive text focuses on a particular subject and attempts to depict the subject in a way that will be clear to readers. Descriptive texts contain many *adjectives* and *adverbs* (i.e., words that give shades of meaning and create a more detailed mental picture for the reader). A descriptive text fails when it is unclear to the reader. A descriptive text will certainly be informative, and the passage may be persuasive and entertaining as well.

Types of Passages

An **expository** passage aims to inform and enlighten readers. The passage is nonfiction and usually centers around a simple, easily defined topic. Since the goal of exposition is to teach, such a passage should be as clear as possible. Often, an expository passage contains helpful *organizing* words, like *first*, *next*, *for example*, and *therefore*. These words keep the reader oriented in the text. Although expository passages do not need to feature colorful language and artful writing, they are often more effective with these features. For a reader, the challenge of expository passages is to maintain steady attention. Expository passages are not always about subjects that will naturally interest a reader, and the writer is often more concerned with clarity and comprehensibility than with engaging the reader. By reading actively, you will ensure a good habit of focus when reading an expository passage.

Review Video: Expository Passages
Visit mometrix.com/academy and enter code: 256515

A **technical** passage is written to describe a complex object or process. Technical writing is common in medical and technological fields, in which complex ideas of mathematics, science, and engineering need to be explained simply and clearly. To ease comprehension, a technical passage usually proceeds in a very logical order. Technical passages often have clear *headings* and *subheadings*, which are used to keep the reader oriented in the text. Additionally, you will find that these passages divide sections up with numbers or letters. Many technical passages look more like an outline than a piece of prose. The amount of jargon or difficult vocabulary will vary in a technical passage depending on the intended audience. As much as possible, technical passages try to avoid language that the reader will have to research in order to understand the message, yet readers will find that jargon cannot always be avoided.

Review Video: A Technical Passage
Visit mometrix.com/academy and enter code: 478923

Writing Devices

Authors will use different stylistic and writing devices to make their meaning clear for readers. One of those devices is comparison and contrast. As mentioned previously, when an author describes the ways in which two things are alike, he or she is **comparing** them. When the author describes the ways in which two things are different, he or she is **contrasting** them.

The "compare and contrast" essay is one of the most common forms in nonfiction. These passages are often signaled with certain words: a comparison may have indicating terms such as *both, same, like, too,* and *as well*; while a contrast may have terms like *but, however, on the other hand, instead,* and *yet.*

Of course, comparisons and contrasts may be **implicit** without using any such signaling language. A single sentence may both compare and contrast. Consider the sentence *Brian and Sheila love ice cream, but Brian prefers vanilla and Sheila prefers strawberry*. In one sentence, the author has described both a similarity (love of ice cream) and a difference (favorite flavor).

> **Review Video: Compare and Contrast**
> Visit mometrix.com/academy and enter code: 798319

One of the most common text structures is **cause and effect**. A cause is an act or event that makes something happen, and an effect is the thing that happens as a result of the cause. A cause-and-effect relationship is not always explicit, but there are some terms in English that signal causes, such as *since, because,* and *due to.*

Furthermore, terms that signal effects include *consequently, therefore,* and *this lead(s) to*. As an example, consider the sentence *Because the sky was clear, Ron did not bring an umbrella*. The cause is the clear sky, and the effect is that Ron did not bring an umbrella.

However, readers may find that sometimes the cause-and-effect relationship will not be clearly noted. For instance, the sentence *He was late and missed the meeting* does not contain any signaling words, but the sentence still contains a cause (he was late) and an effect (he missed the meeting).

Be aware of the possibility for a **single** cause to have **multiple** effects (e.g., *Single cause*: Because you left your homework on the table, your dog engulfs the assignment. *Multiple effects*: As a result, you receive a failing grade; your parents do not allow you to visit your friends; you miss out on the new movie and holding the hand of a potential significant other).

Also, the possibility of a **single** effect to have **multiple** causes (e.g.. *Single effect*: Alan has a fever. *Multiple causes*: An unexpected cold front came through the area, and Alan forgot to take his multi-vitamin to avoid being sick.)

Additionally, an effect can in turn be the cause of another effect, in what is known as a **cause-and-effect chain**. (e.g., As a result of her disdain for procrastination, Lynn prepared for her exam. This led to her passing her test with high marks. Hence, her resume was accepted and her application was approved.)

Another element that impacts a text is the author's point of view. The **point of view** of a text is the perspective from which a passage is told. An author will always have a point of view about a story before he or she draws up a plot line. The author will know what events they want to take place, how they want the characters to interact, and how they want the story to resolve. An author will

also have an **opinion** on the topic or series of events which is presented in the story that is based on their prior experience and beliefs.

Review Video: Point of View
Visit mometrix.com/academy and enter code: 383336

The two main points-of-view that authors use--especially in a work of fiction--are first person and third person. If the narrator of the story is also the main character, or *protagonist*, the text is written in **first-person point of view**. In first person, the author writes from the perspective of *I*. **Third-person point of view** is probably the most common that authors use in their passages. Using third person, authors refer to each character by using *he* or *she*. In third-person omniscient, the narrator is not a character in the story and tells the story of all of the characters at the same time.

Main Ideas and Supporting Details

One of the most important skills in reading comprehension is the identification of **topics** and **main ideas.** There is a subtle difference between these two features. The topic is the subject of a text (i.e., what the text is all about). The main idea, on the other hand, is the most important point being made by the author. The topic is usually expressed in a few words at the most while the main idea often needs a full sentence to be completely defined. As an example, a short passage might have the topic of penguins and the main idea could be written as *Penguins are different from other birds in many ways.*

In most nonfiction writing, the topic and the main idea will be stated **directly** and often appear in a sentence at the very beginning or end of the text. When being tested on an understanding of the author's topic, you may be able to skim the passage for the general idea, by reading only the first sentence of each paragraph. A body paragraph's first sentence is often--but not always--the **main topic sentence** which gives you a summary of the content in the paragraph. However, there are cases in which the reader must figure out an **unstated** topic or main idea. In these instances, you must read every sentence of the text and try to come up with an overarching idea that is supported by each of those sentences.

Note: A thesis statement should not be confused with the main idea of the passage. While the main idea gives a brief, general summary of a text, the thesis statement provides a specific perspective on an issue that the author supports with evidence.

> **Review Video: Topics and Main Ideas**
> Visit mometrix.com/academy and enter code: 407801

Supporting details provide evidence and backing for the main point. In order to show that a main idea is correct, or valid, authors add details that prove their point. All texts contain details, but they are only classified as supporting details when they serve to reinforce some larger point. Supporting details are most commonly found in *informative* and *persuasive* texts. In some cases, they will be clearly indicated with terms like *for example* or *for instance*, or they will be enumerated with terms like *first*, *second*, and *last*. However, you need to be prepared for texts that do not contain those indicators. As a reader, you should consider whether the author's supporting details really back up his or her main point. Supporting details can be factual and correct, yet they may not be relevant to the author's point. Conversely, supporting details can seem pertinent, but they can be ineffective because they are based on opinion or assertions that cannot be proven.

An example of a main idea is: *Giraffes live in the Serengeti of Africa.* A supporting detail about giraffes could be: *A giraffe in this region benefits from a long neck by reaching twigs and leaves on tall trees.* The main idea gives the general idea that the text is about giraffes. The supporting detail gives a specific fact about how the giraffes eat.

> **Review Video: Supporting Details**
> Visit mometrix.com/academy and enter code: 396297

Evaluating a Passage

When reading informational texts, there is importance in understanding the logical conclusion of the author's ideas. **Identifying a logical conclusion** can help you determine whether you agree with the writer or not. Coming to this conclusion is much like making an inference: the approach requires you to combine the information given by the text with what you already know in order to make a logical conclusion. If the author intended the reader to draw a certain conclusion, then you can expect the author's argumentation and detail to be leading in that direction. One way to approach the task of drawing conclusions is to make brief notes of all the points made by the author. When the notes are arranged on paper, they may clarify the logical conclusion. Another way to approach conclusions is to consider whether the reasoning of the author raises any pertinent questions. Sometimes you will be able to draw several conclusions from a passage. On occasion these will be conclusions that were never imagined by the author. Therefore, be aware that these conclusions must be **supported directly by the text**.

> **Review Video: Identifying Logical Conclusions**
> Visit mometrix.com/academy and enter code: 281653

The term **text evidence** refers to information that supports a main point or minor points and can help lead the reader to a conclusion. Information used as text evidence is precise, descriptive, and factual. A main point is often followed by supporting details that provide evidence to back-up a claim. For example, a passage may include the claim that winter occurs during opposite months in the Northern and Southern hemispheres. Text evidence based on this claim may include countries where winter occurs in opposite months along with reasons that winter occurs at different times of the year in separate hemispheres (due to the tilt of the Earth as it rotates around the sun).

> **Review Video: Text Evidence**
> Visit mometrix.com/academy and enter code: 486236

A reader should always be drawing conclusions from the text. Sometimes conclusions are **implied** from written information, and other times the information is **stated directly** within the passage. One should always aim to draw conclusions from information stated within a passage, rather than to draw them from mere implications. At times an author may provide some information and then describe a counterargument. Readers should be alert for direct statements that are subsequently rejected or weakened by the author. Furthermore, you should always read through the entire passage before drawing conclusions. Many readers are trained to expect the author's conclusions at either the beginning or the end of the passage, but many texts do not adhere to this format.

Drawing conclusions from information implied within a passage requires confidence on the part of the reader. **Implications** are things that the author does not state directly, but readers can assume based on what the author does say. Consider the following passage: *I stepped outside and opened my umbrella. By the time I got to work, the cuffs of my pants were soaked.* The author never states that it is raining, but this fact is clearly implied. Conclusions based on implication must be well supported by the text. In order to draw a solid conclusion, readers should have **multiple pieces of evidence**. If readers have only one piece, they must be assured that there is no other possible explanation than their conclusion. A good reader will be able to draw many conclusions from information implied by the text which will be a great help in the exam.

Another helpful tool is the ability to **summarize** the information that you have read in a paragraph or passage format. This process is similar to creating an effective outline. First, a summary should accurately define the **main idea** of the passage though the summary does not need to explain this main idea in exhaustive detail. The summary should continue by laying out the most important **supporting details** or arguments from the passage. All of the significant supporting details should be included, and none of the details included should be irrelevant or insignificant. Also, the summary should accurately report all of these details. Too often, the desire for brevity in a summary leads to the sacrifice of clarity or accuracy. Summaries are often difficult to read because they omit all of the graceful language, digressions, and asides that distinguish great writing. However, an effective summary should contain much the same message as the **original text**.

Paraphrasing is another method that the reader can use to aid in comprehension. When paraphrasing, one puts what they have read into their words by rephrasing what the author has written, or one "translates" all of what the author shared into their words by including as many details as they can.

Responding to a Passage

When reading a good passage, readers are moved to engage actively in the text. One part of being an active reader involves making predictions. A **prediction** is a guess about what will happen next. Readers constantly make predictions based on what they have read and what they already know. Consider the following sentence: *Staring at the computer screen in shock, Kim blindly reached over for the brimming glass of water on the shelf to her side.* The sentence suggests that Kim is agitated, and that she is not looking at the glass that she is going to pick up. So, a reader might predict that Kim is going to knock over the glass. Of course, not every prediction will be accurate: perhaps Kim will pick the glass up cleanly. Nevertheless, the author has certainly created the expectation that the water might be spilled. Predictions are always subject to **revision** as the reader acquires more information.

Review Video: Predictions
Visit mometrix.com/academy and enter code: 437248

Test-taking tip: To respond to questions requiring future predictions, your answers should be based on evidence of past or present behavior.

Readers are often required to understand a text that claims and suggests ideas without stating them directly. An **inference** is a piece of information that is implied but not written outright by the author. For instance, consider the following sentence: *After the final out of the inning, the fans were filled with joy and rushed the field.* From this sentence, a reader can infer that the fans were watching a baseball game and their team won the game.

Readers should take great care to avoid using information beyond the provided passage before making inferences. As you practice with drawing inferences, you will find that they require concentration and attention.

Review Video: Inference
Visit mometrix.com/academy and enter code: 379203

Test-taking tip: While being tested on your ability to make correct inferences, you must look for contextual clues. An answer can be *true* but not *correct*. The contextual clues will help you find the answer that is the best answer out of the given choices. Be careful in your reading to understand the in which a phrase is stated. When asked for the implied meaning of a statement made in the passage, you should immediately locate the statement and read the context in which the statement was made. Also, look for an answer choice that has a similar phrase to the statement in question.

Readers must be able to identify a text's **sequence**, or the order in which things happen. Often, when the sequence is very important to the author, the text is indicated with signal words like *first, then, next,* and *last.* However, a sequence can be merely implied and must be noted by the reader. Consider the sentence *He walked through the garden and gave water and fertilizer to the plants.* Clearly, the man did not walk through the garden before he collected water and fertilizer for the plants. So, the implied sequence is that he first collected water, then he collected fertilizer, next he walked through the garden, and last he gave water or fertilizer as necessary to the plants. Texts do not always proceed in an orderly sequence from first to last. Sometimes they begin at the end and

start over at the beginning. As a reader, you can enhance your understanding of the passage by taking brief notes to clarify the sequence.

Review Video: Sequence
Visit mometrix.com/academy and enter code: 489027

In addition to inference and prediction, readers must often **draw conclusions** about the information they have read. When asked for a *conclusion* that may be drawn, look for critical "hedge" phrases, such as *likely, may, can, will often*, among many others. When you are being tested on this knowledge, remember the question that writers insert into these hedge phrases to cover every possibility. Often an answer will be wrong simply because there is no room for exception. Extreme positive or negative answers (e.g., always or never) are usually not correct. The reader should not use any outside knowledge that is not gathered from the passage to answer the related questions. Correct answers can be derived straight from the passage.

Critical Thinking Skills

OPINIONS, FACTS, AND FALLACIES

Critical thinking skills are mastered through understanding various **types** of writing and the different **purposes** of authors in writing their passages. Every author writes for a purpose. When you understand their purpose and how they accomplish their goal, you will be able to analyze their writing and determine whether or not you agree with their conclusions.

Readers must always be conscious of the distinction between fact and opinion. A **fact** can be subjected to analysis and can be either proved or disproved. An **opinion**, on the other hand, is the author's personal thoughts or feelings which may not be alterable by research or evidence. If the author writes that the distance from New York to Boston is about two hundred miles, then he or she is stating a fact. If an author writes that New York is too crowded, then he or she is giving an opinion because there is no objective standard for overpopulation. An opinion may be indicated by words like *believe*, *think*, or *feel*. Readers must be aware that an opinion may be supported by facts. For instance, the author might give the population density of New York as a reason for an overcrowded population. An opinion supported by fact tends to be more convincing. On the other hand, when authors support their opinions with other opinions, readers should not be persuaded by the argument to any degree.

When you have an argumentative passage, you need to be sure that facts are presented to the reader from **reliable sources**. An opinion is what the author thinks about a given topic. An opinion is not common knowledge or proven by expert sources, instead the information is the personal beliefs and thoughts of the author. To distinguish between fact and opinion, a reader needs to consider the type of source that is presenting information, the information that backs-up a claim, and the author's motivation to have a certain point of view on a given topic.

For example, if a panel of scientists has conducted multiple studies on the effectiveness of taking a certain vitamin, then the results are more likely to be factual than a company that is selling a vitamin and claims that taking the vitamin can produce positive effects. The company is motivated to sell their product, and the scientists are using the scientific method to prove a theory. Remember: if you find sentences that contain phrases such as "I think...", then the statement is an opinion.

> **Review Video: <u>Fact or Opinion</u>**
> Visit mometrix.com/academy and enter code: 870899

In their attempt to persuade, writers often make mistakes in their thinking patterns and writing choices. These patterns and choices are important to understand so you can make an informed decision. Every author has a **point of view**, but authors demonstrate a **bias** when they ignore reasonable counterarguments or distort opposing viewpoints. A bias is evident whenever the author is unfair or inaccurate in his or her presentation. Bias may be intentional or unintentional, and readers should be skeptical of the author's argument. Remember that a biased author may still be correct; however, the author will be correct in spite of his or her bias, not because of the bias. A **stereotype** is like a bias, yet a stereotype is applied specifically to a group or place. Stereotyping is considered to be particularly abhorrent because the practice promotes negative generalizations

57

about people. Readers should be very cautious of authors who stereotype in their writing. These faulty assumptions typically reveal the author's ignorance and lack of curiosity.

Review Video: Bias and Stereotype
Visit mometrix.com/academy and enter code: 644829

Sentence Skills Test

Sentence Correction

Each question includes a sentence with part of it underlined. Your answer choices will offer different ways to **reword** or **rephrase** the underlined portion of the sentence. The first answer choice merely repeats the original underlined text, while the others offer different wording.

These questions will test your ability of correct and effective **expression**. Choose your answer carefully, utilizing the standards of written English, including grammar rules, the proper choice of words and of sentence construction. The correct answer will flow smoothly and be both **clear** and **concise**.

Construction Shift

Each question starts with a sentence that you will be asked to **rewrite**. You will be given a short phrase with which to begin the rewritten sentence, and then asked to select the best phrase to continue, or sometimes even complete, the new sentence so that it retains the meaning of the original sentence.

Choose your answer carefully, utilizing the standards of written English, including grammar rules, the proper choice of words and of sentence construction. The correct answer will flow **smoothly** in a simple, clear, and concise manner.

The best strategy for tackling this part is to read the original sentence and the start of the new sentence you must create, and decide what would be the simplest way to complete the sentence, **before you look at any of the answer choices**. Once you look at the answer choices, it's easy to become confused and second-guess yourself, but 90% of the time, the simplest way you can think of to rewrite the sentence will be among the choices (and will be correct). Typically, the rewriting will involve changing a dependent clause into an independent clause, or vice versa.

Grammar Review

THE EIGHT PARTS OF SPEECH

NOUNS

When you talk about a person, place, thing, or idea, you are talking about **nouns**. The two main types of nouns are **common** and **proper** nouns. Also, nouns can be abstract (i.e., general) or concrete (i.e., specific).

Common nouns are the class or group of people, places, and things (Note: Do not capitalize common nouns). Examples of common nouns:

People: boy, girl, worker, manager

Places: school, bank, library, home

Things: dog, cat, truck, car

Proper nouns are the names of a specific person, place, or thing (Note: Capitalize all proper nouns). Examples of proper nouns:

People: Abraham Lincoln, George Washington, Martin Luther King, Jr.

Places: Los Angeles, California / New York / Asia

Things: Statue of Liberty, Earth*, Lincoln Memorial

*Note: When you talk about the planet that we live on, you capitalize *Earth*. When you mean the dirt, rocks, or land, you lowercase *earth*.

General nouns are the names of conditions or ideas. **Specific nouns** name people, places, and things that are understood by using your senses.

General nouns:

Condition: beauty, strength

Idea: truth, peace

Specific nouns:

People: baby, friend, father

Places: town, park, city hall

Things: rainbow, cough, apple, silk, gasoline

Collective nouns are the names for a person, place, or thing that may act as a whole. The following are examples of collective nouns: *class, company, dozen, group, herd, team,* and *public*.

PRONOUNS

Pronouns are words that are used to stand in for a noun. A pronoun may be grouped as personal, intensive, relative, interrogative, demonstrative, indefinite, and reciprocal.

Personal: *Nominative* is the case for nouns and pronouns that are the subject of a sentence. *Objective* is the case for nouns and pronouns that are an object in a sentence. *Possessive* is the case for nouns and pronouns that show possession or ownership.

Singular

	Nominative	Objective	Possessive
First Person	I	me	my, mine
Second Person	you	you	your, yours
Third Person	he, she, it	him, her, it	his, her, hers, its

Plural

	Nominative	Objective	Possessive
First Person	we	us	our, ours
Second Person	you	you	your, yours
Third Person	they	them	their, theirs

Intensive: I myself, you yourself, he himself, she herself, the (thing) itself, we ourselves, you yourselves, they themselves

Relative: which, who, whom, whose

Interrogative: what, which, who, whom, whose

Demonstrative: this, that, these, those

Indefinite: all, any, each, everyone, either/neither, one, some, several

Reciprocal: each other, one another

> **Review Video: Nouns and Pronouns**
> Visit mometrix.com/academy and enter code: 312073

VERBS

If you want to write a sentence, then you need a verb in your sentence. Without a verb, you have no sentence. The verb of a sentence explains action or being. In other words, the verb shows the subject's movement or the movement that has been done to the subject.

TRANSITIVE AND INTRANSITIVE VERBS

A transitive verb is a verb whose action (e.g., drive, run, jump) points to a receiver (e.g., car, dog, kangaroo). Intransitive verbs do not point to a receiver of an action. In other words, the action of the verb does not point to a subject or object.

Transitive: He plays the piano. | The piano was played by him.

Intransitive: He plays. | John writes well.

A dictionary will let you know whether a verb is transitive or intransitive. Some verbs can be transitive and intransitive.

ACTION VERBS AND LINKING VERBS

An action verb is a verb that shows what the subject is doing in a sentence. In other words, an action verb shows action. A sentence can be complete with one word: an action verb. Linking verbs are intransitive verbs that show a condition (i.e., the subject is described but does no action).

Linking verbs link the subject of a sentence to a noun or pronoun, or they link a subject with an adjective. You always need a verb if you want a complete sentence. However, linking verbs are not able to complete a sentence.

Common linking verbs include *appear, be, become, feel, grow, look, seem, smell, sound,* and *taste*. However, any verb that shows a condition and has a noun, pronoun, or adjective that describes the subject of a sentence is a linking verb.

Action: He sings. | Run! | Go! | I talk with him every day. | She reads.

Linking:

   Incorrect: I am.

   Correct: I am John. | I smell roses. | I feel tired.

Note: Some verbs are followed by words that look like prepositions, but they are a part of the verb and a part of the verb's meaning. These are known as phrasal verbs and examples include *call off, look up*, and *drop off*.

VOICE

Transitive verbs come in active or passive voice. If the subject does an action or receives the action of the verb, then you will know whether a verb is active or passive. When the subject of the sentence is doing the action, the verb is **active voice**. When the subject receives the action, the verb is **passive voice**.

Active: Jon drew the picture. (The subject *Jon* is doing the action of *drawing a picture*.)

Passive: The picture is drawn by Jon. (The subject *picture* is receiving the action from Jon.)

VERB TENSES

A verb tense shows the different form of a verb to point to the time of an action. The present and past tense are shown by changing the verb's form. An action in the present *I talk* can change form for the past: *I talked*. However, for the other tenses, an auxiliary (i.e., helping) verb is needed to show the change in form. These helping verbs include *am, are, is | have, has, had | was, were, will* (or *shall*).

Present: I talk	Present perfect: I have talked
Past: I talked	Past perfect: I had talked
Future: I will talk	Future perfect: I will have talked

Present: The action happens at the current time.

   Example: He *walks* to the store every morning.

To show that something is happening right now, use the progressive present tense: I *am walking*.

Past: The action happened in the past.

Example: He *walked* to the store an hour ago.

Future: The action is going to happen later.

Example: I *will walk* to the store tomorrow.

Present perfect: The action started in the past and continues into the present.

Example: I *have walked* to the store three times today.

Past perfect: The second action happened in the past. The first action came before the second.

Example: Before I walked to the store (Action 2), I *had walked* to the library (Action 1).

Future perfect: An action that uses the past and the future. In other words, the action is complete before a future moment.

Example: When she comes for the supplies (future moment), I *will have walked* to the store (action completed in the past).

CONJUGATING VERBS

When you need to change the form of a verb, you are **conjugating** a verb. The key parts of a verb are first person singular, present tense (dream); first person singular, past tense (dreamed); and the past participle (dreamed). Note: the past participle needs a helping verb to make a verb tense. For example, I *have dreamed* of this day. | I *am dreaming* of this day.

Present Tense: Active Voice

	Singular	Plural
First Person	I dream	We dream
Second Person	You dream	You dream
Third Person	He, she, it dreams	They dream

MOOD

There are three moods in English: the indicative, the imperative, and the subjunctive.

The **indicative mood** is used for facts, opinions, and questions.

Fact: You can do this.

Opinion: I think that you can do this.

Question: Do you know that you can do this?

The **imperative** is used for orders or requests.

Order: You are going to do this!

Request: Will you do this for me?

The **subjunctive mood** is for wishes and statements that go against fact.

Wish: I wish that I were going to do this.

Statement against fact: If I were you, I would do this. (This goes against fact because I am not you. You have the chance to do this, and I do not have the chance.)

The mood that causes trouble for most people is the subjunctive mood. If you have trouble with any of the moods, then be sure to practice.

ADJECTIVES

An adjective is a word that is used to modify a noun or pronoun. An adjective answers a question: *Which one?*, *What kind of?*, or *How many?* . Usually, adjectives come before the words that they modify.

Which one?: The *third* suit is my favorite.

What kind?: The *navy blue* suit is my favorite.

How many?: Can I look over the *four* neckties for the suit?

ARTICLES

Articles are adjectives that are used to mark nouns. There are only three: the **definite** (i.e., limited or fixed amount) article *the*, and the **indefinite** (i.e., no limit or fixed amount) articles *a* and *an*. Note: *An* comes before words that start with a vowel sound (i.e., vowels include *a, e, i, o, u*, and *y*). For example, Are you going to get an **u**mbrella?

Definite: I lost *the* bottle that belongs to me.

Indefinite: Does anyone have *a* bottle to share?

COMPARISON WITH ADJECTIVES

Some adjectives are relative and other adjectives are absolute. Adjectives that are **relative** can show the comparison between things. Adjectives that are **absolute** can show comparison. However, they show comparison in a different way. Let's say that you are reading two books. You think that one book is perfect, and the other book is not exactly perfect. It is <u>not</u> possible for the book to be more perfect than the other. Either you think that the book is perfect, or you think that the book is not perfect.

The adjectives that are relative will show the different degrees of something or someone to something else or someone else. The three degrees of adjectives include positive, comparative, and superlative.

The **positive** degree is the normal form of an adjective.

Example: This work is *difficult*. | She is *smart*.

The **comparative** degree compares one person or thing to another person or thing.

Example: This work is *more difficult* than your work. | She is *smarter* than me.

The **superlative** degree compares more than two people or things.

Example: This is the *most difficult* work of my life. | She is the *smartest* lady in school.

ADVERBS

An adverb is a word that is used to modify a verb, adjective, or another adverb. Usually, adverbs answer one of these questions: *When?*, *Where?*, *How?*, and *Why?*. The negatives *not* and *never* are known as adverbs. Adverbs that modify adjectives or other adverbs **strengthen** or **weaken** the words that they modify.

Examples:

He walks quickly through the crowd.

The water flows smoothly on the rocks.

Note: While many adverbs end in *-ly*, you need to remember that not all adverbs end in *-ly*. Also, some words that end in *-ly* are adjectives, not adverbs. Some examples include: *early, friendly, holy, lonely, silly*, and *ugly*. To know if a word that ends in *-ly* is an adjective or adverb, you need to check your dictionary.

Examples:

He is *never* angry.

You talk *too* loudly.

COMPARISON WITH ADVERBS

The rules for comparing adverbs are the same as the rules for adjectives.

The **positive** degree is the standard form of an adverb.

Example: He arrives soon. | She speaks softly to her friends.

The **comparative** degree compares one person or thing to another person or thing.

Example: He arrives sooner than Sarah. | She speaks more softly than him.

The **superlative** degree compares more than two people or things.

Example: He arrives soonest of the group. | She speaks most softly of any of her friends.

PREPOSITIONS

A preposition is a word placed before a noun or pronoun that shows the relationship between an object and another word in the sentence.

Common prepositions:

about	before	during	on
under	after	beneath	for
over	until	against	between
from	past	up	among
beyond	in	through	with
around	by	of	to
within	at	down	off
toward	without		

Examples:

The napkin is *in* the drawer.

The Earth rotates *around* the Sun.

The needle is *beneath* the haystack.

Can you find me *among* the words?

Review Video: What is a Preposition?
Visit mometrix.com/academy and enter code: 946763

CONJUNCTIONS

Conjunctions join words, phrases, or clauses, and they show the connection between the joined pieces. There are coordinating conjunctions that connect equal parts of sentences. Correlative conjunctions show the connection between pairs. Subordinating conjunctions join subordinate (i.e., dependent) clauses with independent clauses.

COORDINATING CONJUNCTIONS

The coordinating conjunctions include: *and, but, yet, or, nor, for,* and *so*

Examples:

The rock was small, but it was heavy.

She drove in the night, and he drove in the day.

CORRELATIVE CONJUNCTIONS

The correlative conjunctions are: *either...or* | *neither...nor* | *not only... but also*

Examples:

Either you are coming, *or* you are staying. | He ran *not only* three miles, *but also* swam 200 yards.

> **Review Video: Coordinating and Correlative Conjunctions**
> Visit mometrix.com/academy and enter code: 390329

SUBORDINATING CONJUNCTIONS

Common subordinating conjunctions include:

after	since	whenever
although	so that	where
because	unless	wherever
before	until	whether
in order that	when	while

Examples:

I am hungry *because* I did not eat breakfast.

He went home *when* everyone left.

> **Review Video: Subordinating Conjunctions**
> Visit mometrix.com/academy and enter code: 958913

INTERJECTIONS

An interjection is a word for exclamation (i.e., great amount of feeling) that is used alone or as a piece to a sentence. Often, they are used at the beginning of a sentence for an introduction. Sometimes, they can be used in the middle of a sentence to show a change in thought or attitude.

Common Interjections: Hey! | Oh,... | Ouch! | Please! | Wow!

Punctuation

CAPITALIZATION

The rules for capitalization are:

1. Capitalize the first word of a sentence and the first word in a direct quotation
   Examples:
   First Word: *Football* is my favorite sport.
   Direct Quote: She asked, "*What* is your name?"

2. Capitalize proper nouns and adjectives that come from proper nouns
   Examples:
   Proper Noun: My parents are from *Europe.*
   Adjective from Proper Noun: My father is *British,* and my mother is *Italian.*

3. Capitalize the names of days, months, and holidays
   Examples:
   Day: Everyone needs to be here on *Wednesday.*
   Month: I am so excited for *December.*
   Holiday: *Independence Day* comes every July.

4. Capitalize the names on a compass for specific areas, not when they give direction
   Examples:
   Specific Area: James is from the *West.*
   Direction: After three miles, turn *south* toward the highway.

5. Capitalize each word in a title (Note: Articles, prepositions, and conjunctions are not capitalized unless they are the first or last word in the title.)
   Examples:
   Titles: <u>*Romeo and Juliet*</u> is a beautiful drama on love.
   Incorrect: <u>*The Taming Of The Shrew*</u> is my favorite. (Remember that internal prepositions and articles are not capitalized.)

   Note: Books, movies, plays (more than one act), newspapers, magazines, and long musical pieces are put in italics. The two examples of Shakespeare's plays are underlined to show their use as an example.

END PUNCTUATION

PERIODS

Use a period to end all sentences except direct questions, exclamations, and questions.

DECLARATIVE SENTENCE

A declarative sentence gives information or makes a statement.

Examples: I can fly a kite. | The plane left two hours ago.

IMPERATIVE SENTENCE

An imperative sentence gives an order or command.

Examples: You are coming with me. | Bring me that note.

PERIODS FOR ABBREVIATIONS

Examples: 3 P.M. | 2 A.M. | Mr. Jones | Mrs. Stevens | Dr. Smith | Bill Jr. | Pennsylvania Ave.

Note: an abbreviation is a shortened form of a word or phrase.

QUESTION MARKS

Question marks should be used following a direct question. A polite request can be followed by a period instead of a question mark.

Direct Question: What is for lunch today? | How are you? | Why is that the answer?

Polite Requests: Can you please send me the item tomorrow. | Will you please walk with me on the track.

EXCLAMATION MARKS

Exclamation marks are used after a word group or sentence that shows much feeling or has special importance. Exclamation marks should not be overused. They are saved for proper **exclamatory interjections**.

Examples: We're going to the finals! | You have a beautiful car! | That's crazy!

COMMAS

The comma is a punctuation mark that can help you understand connections in a sentence. Not every sentence needs a comma. However, if a sentence needs a comma, you need to put it in the right place. A comma in the wrong place (or an absent comma) will make a sentence's meaning unclear. These are some of the rules for commas:

1. Use a comma before a coordinating conjunction joining independent clauses
   Example: Bob caught three fish, and I caught two fish.
2. Use a comma after an introductory phrase or an adverbial clause
   Examples:
   > *After the final out,* we went to a restaurant to celebrate.
   > *Studying the stars,* I was surprised at the beauty of the sky.
3. Use a comma between items in a series.
   Example: I will bring the turkey, the pie, and the coffee.
4. Use a comma between coordinate adjectives not joined with *and*
   Incorrect: The kind, brown dog followed me home.
   Correct: The *kind, loyal* dog followed me home.
   Not all adjectives are **coordinate** (i.e., equal or parallel). There are two simple ways to know if your adjectives are coordinate. One, you can join the adjectives with *and*: *The kind and loyal dog*. Two, you can change the order of the adjectives: *The loyal, kind dog*.
5. Use commas for interjections and after *yes* and *no* responses
   Examples:
   > **Interjection**: Oh, I had no idea. | Wow, you know how to play this game.
   > **Yes and No**: *Yes,* I heard you. | *No,* I cannot come tomorrow.

6. Use commas to separate nonessential modifiers and nonessential appositives

  Examples:

  Nonessential Modifier: John Frank, who is coaching the team, was promoted today.

  Nonessential Appositive: Thomas Edison, an American inventor, was born in Ohio.

7. Use commas to set off nouns of direct address, interrogative tags, and contrast

  Examples:

  Direct Address: You, *John*, are my only hope in this moment.
  Interrogative Tag: This is the last time, *correct*?
  Contrast: You are my friend, *not my enemy*.

8. Use commas with dates, addresses, geographical names, and titles

  Examples:

  Date: *July 4, 1776*, is an important date to remember.
  Address: He is meeting me at *456 Delaware Avenue, Washington, D.C.,* tomorrow morning.
  Geographical Name: *Paris, France*, is my favorite city.
  Title: John Smith, *Ph. D.,* will be visiting your class today.

9. Use commas to separate expressions like *he said* and *she said* if they come between a sentence of a quote

  Examples:

  "I want you to know," he began, "that I always wanted the best for you."
  "You can start," Jane said, "with an apology."

Review Video: Commas
Visit mometrix.com/academy and enter code: 786797

SEMICOLONS

The semicolon is used to connect major sentence pieces of equal value. Some rules for semicolons include:

1. Use a semicolon between closely connected independent clauses that are not connected with a coordinating conjunction.

  Examples:

  She is outside; we are inside.
  You are right; we should go with your plan.

2. Use a semicolon between independent clauses linked with a transitional word.

  Examples:

  I think that we can agree on this; *however*, I am not sure about my friends.
  You are looking in the wrong places; *therefore*, you will not find what you need.

3. Use a semicolon between items in a series that has internal punctuation.

  Example: I have visited New York, New York; Augusta, Maine; and Baltimore, Maryland.

Review Video: Semicolon Usage
Visit mometrix.com/academy and enter code: 370605

COLONS

The colon is used to call attention to the words that follow it. A colon must come after an independent clause. The rules for colons are as follows:

1. Use a colon after an independent clause to make a list

    Example: I want to learn many languages: Spanish, German, and Italian.

2. Use a colon for explanations or to give a quote

    Examples:

    Quote: He started with an idea: "We are able to do more than we imagine."
    Explanation: There is one thing that stands out on your resume: responsibility.

3. Use a colon after the greeting in a formal letter, to show hours and minutes, and to separate a title and subtitle

    Examples:

    Greeting in a formal letter: Dear Sir: | To Whom It May Concern:
    Time: It is 3:14 P.M.
    Title: The essay is titled "America: A Short Introduction to a Modern Country"

PARENTHESES

Parentheses are used for additional information. Also, they can be used to put labels for letters or numbers in a series. Parentheses should be not be used very often. If they are overused, parentheses can be a distraction instead of a help.

Examples:

Extra Information: The rattlesnake (see Image 2) is a dangerous snake of North and South America.

Series: Include in the email (1) your name, (2) your address, and (3) your question for the author.

QUOTATION MARKS

Use quotation marks to close off direct quotations of a person's spoken or written words. Do not use quotation marks around indirect quotations. An indirect quotation gives someone's message without using the person's exact words. Use **single quotation marks** to close off a quotation inside a quotation.

Direct Quote: Nancy said, "I am waiting for Henry to arrive."

Indirect Quote: Henry said that he is going to be late to the meeting.

Quote inside a Quote: The teacher asked, "Has everyone read 'The Gift of the Magi'?"

Quotation marks should be used around the titles of **short works**: newspaper and magazine articles, poems, short stories, songs, television episodes, radio programs, and subdivisions of books or web sites.

Examples:

"Rip van Winkle" (short story by Washington Irving)

"O Captain! My Captain!" (poem by Walt Whitman)

Quotation marks may be used to set off words that are being used in a different way from a dictionary definition. Also, they can be used to highlight **irony**.

Examples:

The boss warned Frank that he was walking on "thin ice."

(Frank is not walking on real ice. Instead, Frank is being warned to avoid mistakes.)

The teacher thanked the young man for his "honesty."

(Honesty and truth are not always the same thing. In this example, the quotation marks around *honesty* show that the teacher does not believe the young man's explanation.)

> **Review Video: Quotation Marks**
> Visit mometrix.com/academy and enter code: 884918

Note: Periods and commas are put **inside** quotation marks. Colons and semicolons are put **outside** the quotation marks. Question marks and exclamation points are placed inside quotation marks when they are part of a quote. When the question or exclamation mark goes with the whole sentence, the mark is left outside of the quotation marks.

Examples:

Period and comma: We read "The Gift of the Magi," "The Skylight Room," and "The Cactus."

Semicolon: They watched "The Nutcracker"; then, they went home.

Exclamation mark that is a part of a quote: The crowd cheered, "Victory!"

Question mark that goes with the whole sentence: Is your favorite short story "The Tell-Tale Heart"?

APOSTROPHES

An apostrophe is used to show **possession** or the **deletion** of letters in contractions. An apostrophe is not needed with the possessive pronouns *his, hers, its, ours, theirs, whose,* and *yours.*

Singular Nouns: David's car | a book's theme | my brother's board game

Plural Nouns with -*s*: the scissors' handle | boys' basketball

Plural Nouns without -*s*: Men's department | the people's adventure

Review Video: Apostrophes
Visit mometrix.com/academy and enter code: 213068

HYPHENS

The hyphen is used to separate **compound words**. The following are the rules for hyphens:

1. Compound numbers come with a hyphen
   Example: This team needs *twenty-five* points to win the game.
2. Fractions need a hyphen if they are used as an adjective
   Correct: The recipe says that we need a *three-fourths* cup of butter.
   Incorrect: *One-fourth* of the road is under construction.
3. Compound words used as adjectives that come before a noun need a hyphen
   Correct: The *well-fed* dog took a nap.
   Incorrect: The dog was *well-fed* for his nap.
4. To avoid confusion with some words, use a hyphen
   Examples: semi-irresponsible | Re-collect |Re-claim

Note: This is not a complete set of the rules for hyphens. A dictionary is the best tool for knowing if a compound word needs a hyphen.

DASHES

Dashes are used to show a **break** or a **change** in thought in a sentence or to act as parentheses in a sentence. When typing, use two hyphens to make a dash. Do not put a space before or after the dash. The following are the rules for dashes:

1. To set off parenthetical statements or an appositive that has internal punctuation.
   Example: The three trees--oak, pine, and magnolia--are coming on a truck tomorrow.
2. To show a break or change in tone or thought.
   Example: The first question--how silly of me--does not have a correct answer.

Improving Sentences and Paragraphs

SUBJECTS AND PREDICATES

SUBJECTS

Every sentence has two things: a subject and a verb. The **subject** of a sentence names who or what the sentence is all about. The subject may be directly stated in a sentence, or the subject may be the implied *you*.

The **complete subject** has the simple subject and all of the modifiers. To find the complete subject, ask *Who* or *What* and insert the verb to complete the question. The answer is the complete subject. To find the **simple subject**, remove all of the modifiers in the complete subject. When you can find the subject of a sentence, you can correct many problems. These problems include sentence fragments and subject-verb agreement.

Examples:

The small red car is the one that he wants for Christmas.

(The complete subject is *the small red car*.)

The young artist is coming over for dinner.

(The complete subject is *the young artist*.)

> **Review Video: Subjects**
> Visit mometrix.com/academy and enter code: 444771

In **imperative** sentences, the verb's subject is understood (e.g., |You| Run to the store). So, the subject may not be in the sentence. Normally, the subject comes before the verb. However, the subject comes after the verb in sentences that begin with *There are* or *There was*.

Direct:

John knows the way to the park.

(Who knows the way to the park? Answer: John)

The cookies need ten more minutes.

(What needs ten minutes? Answer: The cookies)

By five o' clock, Bill will need to leave.

(Who needs to leave? Answer: Bill)

Remember: The subject can come after the verb.

There are five letters on the table for him.

(What is on the table? Answer: Five letters)

There were coffee and doughnuts in the house.

(What was in the house? Answer: Coffee and doughnuts)

Implied:

Go to the post office for me.

(Who is going to the post office? Answer: You are.)

Come and sit with me, please?

(Who needs to come and sit? Answer: You do.)

PREDICATES

In a sentence, you always have a predicate and a subject. A **predicate** is what remains when you have found the subject. The subject tells what the sentence is about, and the predicate explains or describes the subject.

Think about the sentence: *He sings.* In this sentence, we have a subject (He) and a predicate (sings). This is all that is needed for a sentence to be complete. Would we like more information? Of course, we would like to know more. However, if this all the information that you are given, you have a complete sentence.

Now, let's look at another sentence:

John and Jane sing on Tuesday nights at the dance hall.

What is the subject of this sentence?

Answer: John and Jane.

What is the predicate of this sentence?

Answer: Everything else in the sentence besides John and Jane.

SUBJECT-VERB AGREEMENT

Verbs **agree** with their subjects in number. In other words, *singular* subjects need *singular* verbs. *Plural* subjects need *plural* verbs. Singular is for one person, place, or thing. Plural is for more than one person, place, or thing. Subjects and verbs must also agree in person: first, second, or third. The present tense ending *-s* is used on a verb if its subject is third person singular; otherwise, the verb takes no ending.

> **Review Video: Subject Verb Agreement**
> Visit mometrix.com/academy and enter code: 479190

NUMBER AGREEMENT EXAMPLES:

Single Subject and Verb: *Dan calls home.*

(Dan is one person. So, the singular verb *calls* is needed.)

Plural Subject and Verb: *Dan and Bob call home.*

(More than one person needs the plural verb *call.*)

PERSON AGREEMENT EXAMPLES:

First Person: I *am* walking.

Second Person: You *are* walking.

Third Person: He *is* walking.

PROBLEMS WITH SUBJECT-VERB AGREEMENT

WORDS BETWEEN SUBJECT AND VERB

The joy of my life returns home tonight.

(**Singular Subject**: joy. **Singular Verb**: returns)

The phrase *of my life* does not influence the verb *returns.*

The question that still remains unanswered is "Who are you?"

(**Singular Subject**: question. **Singular Verb**: is)

Don't let the phrase *"that still remains…"* trouble you. The subject *question* goes with *is.*

COMPOUND SUBJECTS

You and Jon are invited to come to my house.

(**Plural Subject**: You and Jon. **Plural Verb**: are)

The pencil and paper belong to me.

(**Plural Subject**: pencil and paper. **Plural Verb**: belong)

SUBJECTS JOINED BY OR AND NOR

Today or tomorrow is the day.

(**Subject**: Today / tomorrow. **Verb**: is)

Stan or Phil wants to read the book.

(**Subject**: Stan / Phil. **Verb**: wants)

Neither the books nor the *pen is* on the desk.

(**Subject**: Books / Pen. **Verb**: is)

Either the blanket or *pillows arrive* this afternoon.

(**Subject**: Blanket / Pillows. **Verb**: arrive)

Note: Singular subjects that are joined with the conjunction *or* need a singular verb. However, when one subject is singular and another is plural, you make the verb agree with the **closer subject**. The example about books and the pen has a singular verb because the pen (singular subject) is closer to the verb.

INDEFINITE PRONOUNS: EITHER, NEITHER, AND EACH
Is either of you ready for the game?

(**Singular Subject**: Either. **Singular Verb**: is)

Each man, woman, and child is unique.

(**Singular Subject**: Each. **Singular Verb**: is)

THE ADJECTIVE EVERY AND COMPOUNDS: EVERYBODY, EVERYONE, ANYBODY, ANYONE
Every day passes faster than the last.

(**Singular Subject**: Every day. **Singular Verb**: passes)

Anybody is welcome to bring a tent.

(**Singular Subject**: Anybody. **Singular Verb**: is)

COLLECTIVE NOUNS
The family eats at the restaurant every Friday night.

(The members of the family are one at the restaurant.)

The team are leaving for their homes after the game.

(The members of the team are leaving as individuals to go to their own homes.)

WHO, WHICH, AND THAT AS SUBJECTS
This is the man who is helping me today.

He is a good man who serves others before himself.

This painting that is hung over the couch is very beautiful.

PLURAL FORM AND SINGULAR MEANING
Some nouns are singular in meaning but plural in form: news, mathematics, physics, and economics.

The news is coming on now.

Mathematics is my favorite class.

Some nouns are always plural in meaning: athletics, gymnastics, scissors, and pants.

Do these pants come with a shirt?

The scissors are for my project.

Note: Look to your dictionary for help when you aren't sure whether a noun with a plural form has a singular or plural meaning.

Addition, Multiplication, Subtraction, and Division are normally singular.

One plus one is two.

Three times three is nine.

COMPLEMENTS

A complement is a noun, pronoun, or adjective that is used to give more information about the verb in the sentence.

DIRECT OBJECTS

A direct object is a noun that takes or receives the **action** of a verb. Remember: a complete sentence does not need a direct object. A sentence needs only a subject and a verb. When you are looking for a direct object, find the verb and ask *who* or *what*.

I took the blanket. (Who or what did I take? *The blanket*)

Jane read books. (Who or what does Jane read? *Books*)

INDIRECT OBJECTS

An indirect object is a word or group of words that show how an action had an **influence** on someone or something. If there is an indirect object in a sentence, then you always have a direct object in the sentence. When you are looking for the indirect object, find the verb and ask *to/for whom or what*.

We taught the old dog a new trick.

(To/For Whom or What was taught? *The old dog*)

I gave them a math lesson.

(To/For Whom or What was given? *Them*)

Predicate Nouns are nouns that modify the subject and finish linking verbs.

My father is a lawyer.

Father is the subject. Lawyer is the predicate noun.

Predicate Adjectives are adjectives that modify the subject and finish linking verbs.

Your mother is patient.

Mother is the subject. Patient is the predicate adjective.

PRONOUN USAGE

Pronoun - Antecedent Agreement - The **antecedent** is the noun that has been replaced by a pronoun. A pronoun and the antecedent agree when they are singular or plural.

Singular agreement: *John* came into town, and *he* played for us.

(The word *He* replaces *John*.)

Plural agreement: *John and Rick* came into town, and *they* played for us.

(The word *They* replaces *John* and *Rick*.)

To know the correct pronoun for a compound subject, try each pronoun **separately** with the verb. Your knowledge of pronouns will tell you which one is correct.

Example:

Bob and (I, me) will be going.

Answer: Bob and I will be going.

Test: (1) *I will be going* or (2) *Me will be going*. The second choice cannot be correct because *me* is not used as a subject of a sentence. Instead, *me* is used as an object.

When a pronoun is used with a noun immediately following (as in "we boys"), try the sentence without the added noun.

Example:

(We/Us) boys played football last year.

Answer: We boys played football last year.

Test: (1) *We* played football last year or (2) *Us* played football last year. Again, the second choice cannot be correct because *us* is not used as a subject of a sentence. Instead, *us* is used as an object.

> **Review Video: Pronoun Usage**
> Visit mometrix.com/academy and enter code: 666500

Pronoun Reference - A pronoun should point clearly to the **antecedent**. Here is how a pronoun reference can be unhelpful if it is not directly stated or puzzling.

Unhelpful: Ron and Jim went to the store, and he bought soda.

(Who bought soda? Ron or Jim?)

Helpful: Jim went to the store, and he bought soda.

(The sentence is clear. Jim bought the soda.)

Personal Pronouns - Some pronouns change their form by their placement in a sentence. A pronoun that is a subject in a sentence comes in the **subjective case**. Pronouns that serve as objects appear in the **objective case**. Finally, the pronouns that are used as possessives appear in the **possessive case**.

Subjective case: *He* is coming to the show.

(The pronoun *He* is the subject of the sentence.)

Objective case: Josh drove *him* to the airport.

(The pronoun *him* is the object of the sentence.)

Possessive case: The flowers are *mine*.

(The pronoun *mine* shows ownership of the flowers.)

Who or whom - Who, a subjective-case pronoun, can be used as a **subject**. *Whom*, an objective case pronoun, can be used as an **object**. The words *who* and *whom* are common in subordinate clauses or in questions.

Subject: He knows who wants to come.

(*Who* is the subject of the verb *wants*.)

Object: He knows whom we want at the party.

(*Whom* is the object of *we want*.)

WORD CONFUSION

Which is used for things only.

Example: John's dog, *which was called Max,* is large and fierce.

That is used for people or things.

Example: Is this the only book *that Louis L'Amour wrote?*

Example: Is Louis L'Amour the author *that wrote Western novels?*

Who is used for people only.

Example: Mozart was the composer *who wrote those operas.*

HOMOPHONES

Homophones are words that sound alike, but they have different **spellings** and **definitions**.

TO, TOO, AND TWO

To can be an adverb or a preposition for showing direction, purpose, and relationship. See your dictionary for the many other ways use *to* in a sentence.

Examples: I went to the store. | I want to go with you.

Too is an adverb that means *also, as well, very, or more than enough.*

Examples: I can walk a mile too. | You have eaten too much.

Two is the second number in the series of numbers (e.g., one (1), two, (2), three (3)...)

Example: You have two minutes left.

THERE, THEIR, AND THEY'RE

There can be an adjective, adverb, or pronoun. Often, *there* is used to show a place or to start a sentence.

> Examples: I went there yesterday. | There is something in his pocket.

Their is a pronoun that is used to show ownership.

> Examples: He is their father. | This is their fourth apology this week.

They're is a contraction of *they are*.

> Example: Did you know that they're in town?

KNEW AND NEW

Knew is the past tense of *know*.

> Example: I knew the answer.

New is an adjective that means something is current, has not been used, or modern.

> Example: This is my new phone.

ITS AND IT'S

Its is a pronoun that shows ownership.

> Example: The guitar is in its case.

It's is a contraction of *it is*.

> Example: It's an honor and a privilege to meet you.

Note: The *h* in honor is silent, so the sound of the vowel *o* must have the article *an*.

YOUR AND YOU'RE

Your is a pronoun that shows ownership.

> Example: This is your moment to shine.

You're is a contraction of you are.

> Example: Yes, you're correct.

AFFECT AND EFFECT

There are two main reasons that **affect** and **effect** are so often confused: 1) both words can be used as either a noun or a verb, and 2) unlike most homophones, their usage and meanings are closely related to each other. Here is a quick rundown of the four usage options:

Affect (n): feeling, emotion, or mood that is displayed

> Example: The patient had a flat *affect*. (i.e., his face showed little or no emotion)

Affect (v): to alter, to change, to influence

> Example: The sunshine *affects* the plant's growth.

Effect (n): a result, a consequence

> Example: What *effect* will this weather have on our schedule?

Effect (v): to bring about, to cause to be

> Example: These new rules will *effect* order in the office.

The noun form of *affect* is rarely used outside of technical medical descriptions, so if a noun form is needed on the test, you can safely select *effect*. The verb form of *effect* is not as rare as the noun form of *affect*, but it's still not all that likely to show up on your test. If you need a verb and you can't decide which to use based on the definitions, choosing *affect* is your best bet.

HOMOGRAPHS

Homographs are words that share the same spelling, and they have multiple meanings. To figure out which meaning is being used, you should be looking for context clues. The context clues give hints to the meaning of the word. For example, the word *spot* has many meanings. It can mean "a place" or "a stain or blot." In the sentence "After my lunch, I saw a spot on my shirt," the word *spot* means "a stain or blot." The context clues of "After my lunch..." and "on my shirt" guide you to this decision.

BANK

(noun): an establishment where money is held for savings or lending

(verb): to collect or pile up

CONTENT

(noun): the topics that will be addressed within a book

(adjective): pleased or satisfied

FINE

(noun): an amount of money that acts a penalty for an offense

(adjective): very small or thin

INCENSE

(noun): a material that is burned in religious settings and makes a pleasant aroma

(verb): to frustrate or anger

LEAD

    (noun): the first or highest position

    (verb): to direct a person or group of followers

OBJECT

    (noun): a lifeless item that can be held and observed

    (verb): to disagree

PRODUCE

    (noun): fruits and vegetables

    (verb): to make or create something

REFUSE

    (noun): garbage or debris that has been thrown away

    (verb): to not allow

SUBJECT

    (noun): an area of study

    (verb): to force or subdue

TEAR

    (noun): a fluid secreted by the eyes

    (verb): to separate or pull apart

CLAUSES

There are two groups of clauses: independent and dependent. Unlike phrases, a clause has a subject and a verb. So, what is the difference between a clause that is independent and one that is dependent? An **independent clause** gives a complete thought. A **dependent clause** does not share a complete thought. Instead, a dependent clause has a subject and a verb, but it needs an independent clause. **Subordinate** (i.e., dependent) clauses look like sentences. They may have a subject, a verb, and objects or complements. They are used within sentences as adverbs, adjectives, or nouns.

Examples:

Independent Clause: I am running outside.

(The sentence has a subject *I* and a verb *am running*.)

Dependent Clause: I am running <u>because I want to stay in shape</u>.

The clause *I am running* is an independent clause. The underlined clause is dependent. Remember: a dependent clause does not give a complete thought. Think about the dependent clause: *because I want to stay in shape.*

Without any other information, you think: So, you want to stay in shape. What are you are doing to stay in shape? Answer: *I am running.*

TYPES OF DEPENDENT CLAUSES

An **adjective clause** is a dependent clause that modifies nouns and pronouns. Adjective clauses begin with a relative pronoun (*who, whose, whom, which,* and *that*) or a relative adverb (*where, when,* and *why*).

Also, adjective clauses come after the noun that the clause needs to explain or rename. This is done to have a clear connection to the independent clause.

Examples:

I learned the reason *why I won the award.*

This is the place *where I started my first job.*

An adjective clause can be an essential or nonessential clause. An essential clause is very important to the sentence. **Essential clauses** explain or define a person or thing. **Nonessential clauses** give more information about a person or thing. However, they are not necessary to the sentence.

Examples:

Essential: A person *who works hard at first* can rest later in life.

Nonessential: Neil Armstrong, *who walked on the moon,* is my hero.

An **adverb clause** is a dependent clause that modifies verbs, adjectives, and other adverbs. To show a clear connection to the independent clause, put the adverb clause immediately before or after the independent clause. An adverb clause can start with *after, although, as, as if, before, because, if, since, so, so that, unless, when, where,* or *while.*

Examples:

When you walked outside, I called the manager.

I want to go with you *unless you want to stay.*

A **noun clause** is a dependent clause that can be used as a subject, object, or complement. Noun clauses can begin with *how, that, what, whether, which, who,* or *why.* These words can also come with an adjective clause.

Remember that the entire clause makes a noun or an adjective clause, not the word that starts a clause. So, be sure to look for more than the word that begins the clause. To show a clear connection to the independent clause, be sure that a noun clause comes after the verb. The exception is when the noun clause is the subject of the sentence.

Examples:

The fact *that you were alone* alarms me.

What you learn from each other depends on your honesty with others.

PHRASES

A phrase is not a complete sentence. So, a phrase cannot be a statement and cannot give a complete thought. Instead, a phrase is a group of words that can be used as a noun, adjective, or adverb in a sentence. Phrases strengthen sentences by adding **explanation** or **renaming** something.

<u>Prepositional Phrases</u> - A phrase that can be found in many sentences is the prepositional phrase. A prepositional phrase begins with a preposition and ends with a noun or pronoun that is used as an object. Normally, the prepositional phrase works as an **adjective** or an **adverb**.

Examples:

> The picnic is *on the blanket.*
>
> I am sick *with a fever* today.
>
> *Among the many flowers*, a four-leaf clover was found by John.

VERBALS AND VERBAL PHRASES

A verbal looks like a verb, but it is not used as a verb. Instead, a verbal is used as a noun, adjective, or adverb. Be careful with verbals. They do **not** replace a verb in a sentence.

> Correct: Walk a mile daily.
>
> (*Walk* is the verb of this sentence. As in, "*You* walk a mile daily.")
>
> Incorrect: To walk a mile.
>
> (*To walk* is a type of verbal. But, verbals cannot be a verb for a sentence.)

A **verbal phrase** is a verb form that does not function as the verb of a clause. There are three major types of verbal phrases: participial, gerund, and infinitive phrases.

Participles - A participle is a verbal that is used as an adjective. The present participle always ends with *-ing*. Past participles end with *-d, -ed, -n,* or *-t.*

> Examples: Verb: *dance* | Present Participle: *dancing* | Past Participle: *danced*

Participial phrases are made of a participle and any complements or modifiers. Often, they come right after the noun or pronoun that they modify.

Examples:

> *Shipwrecked on an island*, the boys started to fish for food.
>
> *Having been seated for five hours*, we got out of the car to stretch our legs.
>
> *Praised for their work*, the group accepted the first-place trophy.

Gerunds - A gerund is a verbal that is used as a noun. Gerunds can be found by looking for their *-ing* endings. However, you need to be careful that you have found a gerund, not a present participle. Since gerunds are nouns, they can be used as a subject of a sentence and the object of a verb or preposition.

Gerund Phrases are built around present participles (i.e., *-ing* endings to verbs) and they are always used as nouns. The gerund phrase has a gerund and any complements or modifiers.

Examples:

We want to be known for *teaching the poor*. (Object of Preposition)

Coaching this team is the best job of my life. (Subject)

We like *practicing our songs* in the basement. (Object of the verb: *like*)

Infinitives - An infinitive is a verbal that can be used as a noun, an adjective, or an adverb. An infinitive is made of the basic form of a verb with the word *to* coming before the verb.

Infinitive Phrases are made of an infinitive and all complements and modifiers. They are used as nouns, adjectives, or adverbs.

Examples:

To join the team is my goal in life. (Noun)

The animals have enough food *to eat for the night*. (Adjective)

People lift weights *to exercise their muscles*. (Adverb)

APPOSITIVE PHRASES

An appositive is a word or phrase that is used to explain or rename nouns or pronouns. In a sentence they can be noun phrases, prepositional phrases, gerund phrases, or infinitive phrases.

Examples:

Terriers, *hunters at heart*, have been dressed up to look like lap dogs.

(The phrase *hunters at heart* renames the noun *terriers*.)

His plan, *to save and invest his money*, was proven as a safe approach.

(The italicized infinitive phrase renames the plan.)

Appositive phrases can be essential or nonessential. An appositive phrase is essential if the person, place, or thing being described or renamed is too general.

Essential: Two Founding Fathers George Washington and Thomas Jefferson served as presidents.

Nonessential: George Washington and Thomas Jefferson, two Founding Fathers, served as presidents.

ABSOLUTE PHRASES

An absolute phrase is a phrase with a participle that comes after a noun. The absolute phrase is never the subject of a sentence. Also, the phrase does not explain or add to the meaning of a word in a sentence. Absolute phrases are used *independently* from the rest of the sentence. However, they are still phrases, and phrases cannot give a complete thought.

Examples:

The alarm ringing, he pushed the snooze button.

The music paused, she continued to dance through the crowd.

Note: Appositive and absolute phrases can be confusing in sentences. So, don't be discouraged if you have a difficult time with them.

SENTENCE STRUCTURES

The four major types of sentence structure are:

1. **Simple Sentences** - Simple sentences have one independent clause with no subordinate clauses. A simple sentence can have compound elements (e.g., a compound subject or verb).

    Examples:

    Judy watered the lawn. (Singular Subject & Singular Predicate)

    Judy and Alan watered the lawn. (Compound Subject: Judy and Alan)

2. **Compound Sentences** - Compound sentences have two or more independent clauses with no dependent clauses. Usually, the independent clauses are joined with a comma and a coordinating conjunction, or they can be joined with a semicolon.
    Example:

    The time has come, and we are ready.

    I woke up at dawn; then I went outside to watch the sun rise.

3. **Complex Sentences** - A complex sentence has one independent clause and one or more dependent clauses.
    Examples:

    Although he had the flu, Harry went to work.

    Marcia got married after she finished college.

4. **Compound-Complex Sentences** - A compound-complex sentence has at least two independent clauses and at least one dependent clause.
    Examples:

    John is my friend who went to India, and he brought souvenirs for us.

    You may not know, but we heard the music that you played last night.

Review Video: Sentence Structure
Visit mometrix.com/academy and enter code: 700478

SENTENCE FRAGMENTS

A part of a sentence should not be treated like a complete sentence. A sentence must be made of at least one **independent clause**. An independent clause has a subject and a verb. Remember that the independent clause can stand alone as a sentence. Some **fragments** are independent clauses that begin with a subordinating word (e.g., as, because, so, etc.). Other fragments may not have a subject, a verb, or both.

A sentence fragment can be **repaired** in several ways. One way is to put the fragment with a neighbor sentence. Another way is to be sure that punctuation is not needed. You can also turn the fragment into a sentence by adding any missing pieces. Sentence fragments are allowed for writers who want to show off their art. However, for your exam, sentence fragments are not allowed.

Fragment: Because he wanted to sail for Rome.

Correct: He dreamed of Europe because he wanted to sail for Rome.

RUN-ON SENTENCES

Run-on sentences are independent clauses that have not been joined by a conjunction. When two or more independent clauses appear in one sentence, they must be **joined** in one of these ways:

1. Correction with a comma and a coordinating conjunction.
    Incorrect: I went on the trip and I had a good time.
    Correct: I went on the trip, and I had a good time.
2. Correction with a semicolon, a colon, or a dash. Used when independent clauses are closely related and their connection is clear without a coordinating conjunction.
    Incorrect: I went to the store and I bought some eggs.
    Correct: I went to the store; I bought some eggs.
3. Correction by separating sentences. This correction may be used when both independent clauses are long. Also, this can be used when one sentence is a question and one is not.
    Incorrect: The drive to New York takes ten hours it makes me very tired.
    Correct: The drive to New York takes ten hours. So, I become very tired.
4. Correction by changing parts of the sentence. One way is to turn one of the independent clauses into a phrase or subordinate clause.
    Incorrect: The drive to New York takes ten hours it makes me very tired.
    Correct: During the ten-hour drive to New York, I become very tired.

Note: Normally, one of these choices will be a clear correction to a run-on sentence. The fourth way can be the best correction but needs the most work.

Review Video: Fragments and Run-on Sentences
Visit mometrix.com/academy and enter code: 541989

DANGLING AND MISPLACED MODIFIERS

DANGLING MODIFIERS

A dangling modifier is a verbal phrase that does not have a **clear connection** to a word. A dangling modifier can also be a dependent clause (the subject and/or verb are not included) that does not have a clear connection to a word.

Examples:

Dangling: *Reading each magazine article*, the stories caught my attention.

Corrected: Reading each magazine article, *I* was entertained by the stories.

In this example, the word *stories* cannot be modified by *Reading each magazine article*. People can read, but stories cannot read. So, the pronoun *I* is needed for the modifying phrase *Reading each magazine article*.

Dangling: Since childhood, my grandparents have visited me for Christmas.

Corrected: Since childhood, I have been visited by my grandparents for Christmas.

In this example, the dependent adverb clause *Since childhood* cannot modify grandparents. So, the pronoun *I* is needed for the modifying adverb clause.

MISPLACED MODIFIERS

In some sentences, a **modifier** can be put in more than one place. However, you need to be sure that there is no confusion about which word is being explained or given more detail.

Incorrect: He read the book to a crowd that was filled with beautiful pictures.

Correct: He read the book that was filled with beautiful pictures to a crowd.

The crowd is not filled with pictures. The book is filled with pictures.

Incorrect: John only ate fruits and vegetables for two weeks.

Correct: John ate *only* fruits and vegetables for two weeks.

John may have done nothing else for two weeks but eat fruits and vegetables and sleep. However, it is reasonable to think that John had fruits and vegetables for his meals. Then, he continued to work on other things.

SPLIT INFINITIVES

A split infinitive occurs when a modifying word comes between the word *to* and the verb that pairs with *to*.

Example: To *clearly* explain vs. *To explain* clearly | To *softly* sing vs. *To sing* softly

Though still considered improper by some, split infinitives may provide better clarity and simplicity than the alternatives. As such, avoiding them should not be considered a universal rule.

DOUBLE NEGATIVES

Standard English allows **two negatives** when a **positive** meaning is intended. For example, "The team was not displeased with their performance." Double negatives that are used to emphasize negation are not part of Standard English.

Negative modifiers (e.g., never, no, and not) should not be paired with other negative modifiers or negative words (e.g., none, nobody, nothing, or neither). The modifiers *hardly, barely*, and *scarcely* are also considered negatives in Standard English. So, they should not be used with other negatives.

PARALLELISM AND SUBORDINATION

PARALLELISM

Parallel structures are used in sentences to highlight similar ideas and to connect sentences that give similar information. **Parallelism** pairs parts of speech, phrases, or clauses together with a matching piece. To write, *I enjoy reading and to study* would be incorrect. An infinitive does not match with a gerund. Instead, you should write *I enjoy reading and studying*.

Be sure that you continue to use certain words (e.g., articles, linking verbs, prepositions, infinitive sign (to), and the introductory word for a dependent clause) in sentences.

Incorrect: Will you bring the paper and pen with you?
Correct: Will you bring *the* paper and *a* pen with you?

Incorrect: The animals can come to eat and play.
Correct: The animals can come *to* eat and *to* play.

Incorrect: You are the person who remembered my name and cared for me.
Correct: You are the person *who* remembered my name and *who* cared for me.

SUBORDINATION

When two items are not equal to each other, you can join them by making the more important piece an **independent clause**. The less important piece can become **subordinate**. To make the less important piece subordinate, you make it a phrase or a dependent clause. The piece of more importance should be the one that readers want or will need to remember.

Example:

(1) The team had a perfect regular season. (2) The team lost the championship.

Despite having a perfect regular season, *the team lost the championship*.

FINAL NOTES

CONTEXT CLUES

To decide on the best answer, you can use context clues as you read through the answer choices. **Key words** in the sentence will allow you to decide which answer choice is the best to fill in the blank.

Example: Archeology has shown that some of the ruins of the ancient city of Babylon are approximately 500 years <u>as old as their supposed</u> Mesopotamian predecessors.

    a. as old as their supposed
    b. older than their supposed

In this example, the key word is *supposed*. Archaeology would confirm that the predecessors to Babylon were more ancient or disprove that supposition. Since supposed was used, the word implies that archaeology had disproved the accepted belief. So, this would make Babylon older. Thus, answer choice B correct.

Furthermore, the use of *500 years* in the sentence can rule out answer choice A. Years are used to show absolute or relative age. If two objects are as old as each other, then years are not necessary to describe that relationship. So, you could say, "The ancient city of Babylon is approximately as old as their supposed Mesopotamian predecessors." So, the term *500 years* is not needed in the sentence.

WATCH OUT FOR SIMPLICITY

When your answer choices seem **simple**, you need to be careful with the question. Don't pick an answer choice because one choice is long or complicated. A simple or short sentence can be correct. However, not every simple or short sentence will be correct. An answer that is simple and does not make sense may not be correct.

The phrases *of which [...] are* in the below examples are wordy and unnecessary. They should be removed. You can place a colon after the words *sport* and *following*.

Examples:

      a. There are many benefits to running as a sport, *of which the top advantages are*:
      b. The necessary school supplies were the following, *of which a few are*:

Essay

BRAINSTORM

Spend the first three to five minutes **brainstorming** for ideas. Write down any ideas that you might have on the topic. The purpose is to pull any helpful information from the depths of your memory. In this stage, anything goes down on scratch paper regardless of how good or bad the idea may seem at first glance. Use the provided scratch paper to put down your ideas.

STRENGTH THROUGH DIFFERENT VIEWPOINTS

The best papers will contain several examples and mature reasoning. As you brainstorm, you should consider different **perspectives**. There are more than two sides to every topic. In an argument, there are countless perspectives that can be considered. On any topic, different groups are impacted and many reach the same conclusion or position. Yet, they reach the same conclusion through different paths. Before writing your essay, try to *see* the topic through as many different *eyes* as you can.

In addition, you don't have to use information on how the topic impacts others. You can draw from your own experience as you wish. If you prefer to use a **personal narrative**, then explain the experience and your emotions from that moment. Anything that you've seen in your community can be expanded upon to round out your position on the topic.

Once you have finished with your creative flow, you need to stop and review what you brainstormed. *Which idea allowed you to come up with the most supporting information?* Be sure to pick an angle that will allow you to have a thorough **coverage** of the prompt.

Every garden of ideas has weeds. The ideas that you brainstormed are going to be random pieces of information of different values. Go through the pieces carefully and pick out the ones that are the best. The best ideas are **strong points** that will be easy to write a paragraph in response.

Now, you have your main ideas that you will focus on. So, align them in a **sequence** that will flow in a smooth, sensible path from point to point. With this approach, readers will go smoothly from one idea to the next in a reasonable order. Readers want an essay that has a sense of continuity (i.e., Point 1 to Point 2 to Point 3 and so on).

START YOUR ENGINES

Now, you have a logical **flow** of the main ideas for the start of your essay. Begin by expanding on the first point, then move to your second point. **Pace** yourself. Don't spend too much time on any one of the ideas that you are expanding on. You want to have time for all of them. Make sure that you watch your time. If you have twenty minutes left to write out your ideas and you have four ideas, then you can only use five minutes per idea. Writing so much information in so little time can be an intimidating task. Yet, when you pace yourself, you can get through all of your points. If you find that you are falling behind, then you can remove one of your weaker arguments. This will allow you to give enough support to your remaining paragraphs.

Once you finish expanding on an idea, go back to your brainstorming session where you wrote out your ideas. You can scratch through the ideas as you write about them. This will let you see what you need to write about next and what you have left to cover.

Your **introductory paragraph** should have several easily identifiable features.

- First, the paragraph should have a quick **description** or paraphrasing of the topic. Use your own words to briefly explain what the topic is about.
- Second, you should list your **writing points**. What are the main ideas that you came up with earlier? If someone was to read only your introduction, they should be able to get a good summary of the entire paper.
- Third, you should explain your opinion of the topic and give an explanation for why you feel that way. What is your decision or **conclusion** on the topic?

Each of your following paragraphs should develop one of the points listed in the main paragraph. Use your personal experience and knowledge to support each of your points. Examples should back up everything.

Once you have finished expanding on each of your main points, you need to conclude your essay. **Summarize** what you written in a conclusion paragraph. Explain once more your argument on the prompt and review why you feel that way in a few sentences. At this stage, you have already backed up your statements. So, there is no need to do that again. You just need to refresh your readers on the main points that you made in your essay.

DON'T PANIC

Whatever you do during essay, do not **panic**. When you panic, you will put fewer words on the page and your ideas will be weak. Therefore, panicking is not helpful. If your mind goes blank when you see the prompt, then you need to take a deep breath. Force yourself to go through the steps listed above: brainstorm and put anything on scratch paper that comes to mind.

Also, don't get **clock fever**. You may be overwhelmed when you're looking at a page that has is mostly blank. Your mind is full of random thoughts and feeling confused, and the clock is ticking down faster. You have already brainstormed for ideas. Therefore, you don't have to keep coming up with ideas. If you're running out of time and you have a lot of ideas that you haven't written down, then don't be afraid to make some cuts. Start picking the best ideas that you have left and expand on them. Don't feel like you have to write on all of your ideas.

A short paper that is **well written** and **well organized** is better than a long paper that is poorly written and poorly organized. Don't keep writing about a subject just to add sentences and avoid repeating a statement or idea that you have explained already. The goal is 1 to 2 pages of quality writing. That is your target, but you should not mess up your paper by trying to get there. You want to have a natural end to your work without having to cut something short. If your essay is a little long, then that isn't a problem as long as your ideas are clear and flow well from paragraph to paragraph. Remember to expand on the ideas that you identified in the brainstorming session.

Leave time at the end (at least three minutes) to go back and **check** over your work. Reread and make sure that everything you've written makes sense and flows well. Clean up any spelling or grammar mistakes. Also, go ahead and erase any brainstorming ideas that you weren't able to include. Then, clean up any extra information that you might have written that doesn't fit into your paper.

As you proofread, make sure that there aren't any fragments or run-ons. Check for sentences that are too short or too long. If the sentence is too short, then look to see if you have a specific subject and an active verb. If it is too long, then break up the long sentence into two sentences. Watch out for any "big words" that you may have used. Be sure that you are using difficult words correctly.

Don't misunderstand; you should try to increase your vocabulary and use difficult words in your essay. However, your focus should be on developing and expressing ideas in a **clear** and **precise** way.

THE SHORT OVERVIEW

Depending on your preferences and personality, the essay may be your hardest or your easiest section. You are required to go through the entire process of writing a paper in a limited amount of time, which is very challenging.

Stay focused on each of the steps for brainstorming. Go through the process of **creative flow** first. You can start by generating ideas about the prompt. Next, organize those ideas into a smooth flow. Then, pick out the ideas that are the best from your list.

Create a recognizable **essay structure** in your paper. Start with an introduction that explains what you have decided to argue. Then, choose your main points. Use the body paragraphs to touch on those main points and have a conclusion that wraps up the topic.

Save a few moments to go back and **review** what you have written. Clean up any minor mistakes that you might have made and make those last few critical touches that can make a huge difference. Finally, be proud and confident of what you have written!

Practice Test

Sentence Skills

Directions for questions 1–10

Select the best version of the underlined part of the sentence. The first choice is the same as the original sentence. If you think the original sentence is best, choose the first answer.

1. Several theories <u>about what caused dinosaurs to have extinction exist</u>, but scientists are still unable to reach a concrete conclusion.

    A. about what caused dinosaurs to have extinction exist
    B. about what caused dinosaurs to become extinct exist
    C. about the causes of the dinosaur extinction exists
    D. in regards to the extinction cause of dinosaurs exist

2. <u>Although most persons</u> prefer traditional pets like cats and dogs, others gravitate towards exotic animals like snakes and lizards.

    A. Although most persons
    B. Because most people
    C. While most people
    D. Maybe some persons

3. It is important that software companies offer tech support <u>to customers who are encountering problems</u>.

    A. to customers who are encountering problems
    B. because not all customers encounter problems
    C. with customers who encounter problems
    D. to customer who is encountering difficulties

4. The fact <u>that children eat high fat diets and watch excessive amount of television are a cause of concern</u> for many parents.

    A. that children eat high fat diets and watch excessive amount of television are a cause of concern
    B. the children eat high fat diets and watches excessive amount of television are a cause of concern
    C. is children eat high fat diets and watch excessive amount of television is a cause for concern
    D. that children eat high fat diets and watch excessive amounts of television is a cause for concern

5. <u>Contrarily to popular beliefs,</u> bats do not actually entangle themselves in the hair of humans on purpose.

    A. Contrarily to popular beliefs
    B. Contrary to popular belief
    C. Contrary to popularity belief
    D. Contrary to popular believing

6. <u>Considering how long ago the Ancient Egyptians lived, it's amazing</u> we know anything about them at all.

    A. Considering how long ago the Ancient Egyptians lived, it's amazing

    B. Consider how long the Ancient Egyptians lived, it's amazing

    C. Considering for how long the Ancient Egyptians lived, its amazing

    D. Considering, how long ago the Ancient Egyptians lived, its amazing

7. <u>Because technology has constantly changed</u>, those employed in the IT industry must learn new skills continuously.

    A. Because technology has constantly changed

    B. Because technology is constantly changing

    C. Even though technology is changing

    D. Despite the fact that technology has changed

8. <u>To mix, shade, and highlighting</u> are essential skills that every beginning artist must master.

    A. To mix, shade, and highlighting

    B. Mix, shade, and highlighting

    C. To mixing, shading, and highlighting

    D. Mixing, shading, and highlighting

9. The growing problem of resistance to antibiotics can be attributed, in part, <u>to the fact that they are prescribed unnecessarily</u>.

    A. to the fact that they are prescribed unnecessarily

    B. in the facts that they are prescribed unnecessarily

    C. to the fact that they are prescribing unnecessarily

    D. with the facts that they are being prescribed unnecessarily.

10. <u>A key challenges facing university graduates</u> searching for employment is that most have limited work experience.

    A. A key challenges facing university graduates

    B. Key challenge faced by university graduates

    C. A key challenge facing university graduates

    D. Key challenges facing university's graduates

Directions for questions 11–20

Rewrite the sentence in your head following the directions given below. Keep in mind that your new sentence should be well written and should have essentially the same meaning as the original sentence.

11. Mitosis is the process of cell division, and if there are errors during this process, it can result in serious complications.

Rewrite, beginning with

Serious complications can result

The next words will be

    A. during the process of cell division
    B. if there are errors during the process
    C. in the process of mitosis
    D. when this process leads to errors

12. It was a very tough decision, but Sharon finally decided after much consideration to study biology at Yale University.

Rewrite, beginning with

After much consideration

The next words will be

    A. Sharon finally decided to study
    B. it was a very tough decision
    C. Sharon studied biology at Yale University
    D. a very tough study was decided

13. Small business owners must compete with larger stores by providing excellent service, because department store prices are simply too low for owners of small businesses to match them.

Rewrite, beginning with

Prices in department stores are simply too low for owners of small businesses to match them,

The next words will be

    A. so small business owners must
    B. while small business owners must
    C. when small business owners must
    D. because small business owners must

14. Ants are fascinating creatures, and some of their unique characteristics are their strength, organizational skills, and construction talents.

Rewrite, beginning with

Strength, organizational skills, and construction talents

The next words will be

    A. are some of the unique characteristics
    B. are possessed by fascinating creatures
    C. of ants are fascinating characteristics
    D. are unique characteristics of their

15. Many people do not regularly wear their seatbelts, even though law enforcement professionals warn motorists about the dangers of not doing so.

Rewrite, beginning with

Despite warnings by law enforcement professionals

The next words will be

    A. motorists ignore the dangers of not doing so
    B. many people do not regularly wear their seatbelts
    C. about the people who don't wear seatbelts
    D. even though motorists do not wear seatbelts

16. The wolverine is an incredibly strong animal that is actually closely related to weasels, and not, as many people believe, related to wolves.

Rewrite, beginning with

Many people believe the wolverine is

The next words will be

    A. closely related to weasels
    B. an incredibly strong animal
    C. related to wolves
    D. a weasel, but they are actually

17. Advertising aimed at children is of greater concern than that aimed towards adults because children are more likely to internalize the messages presented in print and television ads.

Rewrite, beginning with

Because children are more likely to internalize the messages presented in ads,

The next words will be

    A. advertising aimed at children
    B. advertising aimed towards adults
    C. is of greater concern than that
    D. print and television advertisements

18. Increasing housing and fuel costs in the United States have caused many people to accumulate high levels of consumer and credit debt, and this is particularly true for people who have limited incomes.

Rewrite, beginning with

Many people have accumulated high levels of debt

The next words will be

    A. for those who have limited income
    B. mainly in the United States
    C. due to increasing housing and fuel costs
    D. for consumer and credit

19. People and companies who sell products online often charge a lot for shipping, which is why even though it is possible to find low prices online, customers may not be saving as much money as they think.

Rewrite, beginning with

<u>Customers may not be saving as much money as they think</u>

The next words will be

    A. which is why it is possible to charge for shipping
    B. because people and companies who sell
    C. because it is possible to find low prices
    D. when people and companies shop online

20. In the world of stock option trading, purchasing a put gives an individual the right to sell shares, so they will likely profit if the value of a company's stock decreases, but not if it increases.

Rewrite, beginning with

<u>An individual will profit if the value of a company's stock decreases</u>

The next words will be

    A. in the world of stock option trading
    B. giving them a right to sell shares
    C. or if it increases
    D. if he purchases a put

Reading Comprehension

Directions for questions 1–10

Read the statement or passage and then choose the best answer to the question. Answer the question based on what is stated or implied in the statement or passage.

1. During the 1970s, a new type of pet became popular in North America. Although they were actually just brine shrimp, they were marketed as "Sea Monkeys." They don't actually look like monkeys at all, but were branded as such due to their long tails. When sea monkeys first began to be sold in the United States, they were sold under the brand name "Instant Life." Later, when they became known as sea monkeys, the cartoon drawings that were featured in comic books showed creatures that resembled humans more than shrimp. The creative marketing of these creatures can only be described as genius, and at the height of their popularity in the 1970s, they could be found in as many as one in five homes.

Based on the information in the passage, it can be inferred that

    A. Sea monkeys were more popular when they were marketed as "instant life."
    B. Sea monkeys wouldn't have been as popular if they had been marketed as "brine shrimp."
    C. Most people thought they were actually purchasing monkeys that lived in the sea.
    D. There are more homes today that have sea monkeys than there were in the 1970s.

2. Before the battle between CDs and MP3s, there was a rivalry during the 1960s between the four-track and the eight-track tape. Four-track tapes were invented in the early 1960s by Earl Muntz, an entrepreneur from California. Later, Bill Lear designed the eight-track tape. This latter invention was similar in size to the four-track tape, but it could store and play twice as many songs. Lear had close ties with the motor company Ford, and he convinced them to include eight-track players in their vehicles, which definitely helped the eight-track tape to achieve a high level of popularity. Soon after, they began being used in homes, and the four-track tape all but disappeared.

The main difference between the four-track and eight-track tape was

    A. The four-track tape was much larger than the eight-track tape.
    B. The eight-track tape cost a lot more to produce than the four-track tape.
    C. The eight-track tape could hold more songs than the four-track tape.
    D. The four-track tape was usually included in Ford vehicles.

3. It is natural for humans to have fears, but when those fears are completely irrational and begin to interfere with everyday activities they are known as phobias. Agoraphobia is a serious phobia, and it can be devastating for those who suffer from it. Contrary to popular belief, agoraphobia is not simply a fear of open spaces. Rather, the agoraphobic fears being in a place that he feels is unsafe. Depending on the severity of the problem, the agoraphobic might fear going to the mall, walking down the street, or even walking to the mailbox. Often, the agoraphobic will view his home as the safest possible place to be, and he may even be reluctant to leave his house. Treatments for this condition include medication and behavioral therapy.

An agoraphobic would feel safest

    A. In their yard.
    B. In their house.
    C. In a mall.
    D. On the sidewalk.

4. The butterfly effect is a somewhat poorly understood mathematical concept, primarily because it is interpreted and presented incorrectly by the popular media. It refers to systems, and how initial conditions can influence the ultimate outcome of an event. The best way to understand the concept is through an example. You have two rubber balls. There are two inches between them, and you release them. Where will they end up? Well, that depends. If they're in a sloped, sealed container, they will end up two inches away from each other at the end of the slope. If it's the top of a mountain, however, they may end up miles away from each other. They could bounce off rocks; one could get stuck in a snow bank while the other continues down the slope; one could enter a river and get swept away. The fact that even a tiny initial difference can have a significant overall impact is known as the butterfly effect.

The purpose of this passage is

    A. To discuss what could happen to two rubber balls released on top of a mountain.
    B. To show why you can predict what will happen to two objects in a sloped, sealed container.
    C. To discuss the primary reason why the butterfly effect is a poorly understood concept.
    D. To give an example of how small changes at the beginning of an event can have large effects.

5. Wells provide water for drinking, bathing, and cleaning to many people across the world. When wells are being dug, there are several issues that must be taken into account to minimize the chance of potential problems down the road. First, it's important to be aware that groundwater levels differ, depending on the season. In general, groundwater levels will be higher during the winter. So if a well is being dug during the winter, it should be deep enough to remain functional during the summer, when water levels are lower. Well water that is used is replaced by melting snow and rain. If the well owners are using the water faster than it can be replaced, however, the water levels will be lowered. The only way to remedy this, aside from waiting for the groundwater to be replenished naturally, is to deepen the well.

From this passage, it can be concluded that

    A. It is better to have a well that is too deep than one that is too shallow.
    B. Most well owners will face significant water shortages every year.
    C. Most people who dig wells during the winter do not make them deep enough.
    D. Well water is safe to use for bathing and cleaning, but is not suitable for drinking.

6. Today's low-fat craze has led many people to assume that all fats are unhealthy, but this is simply not the case. Fat is an essential component of any healthy diet because it provides energy and helps the body process nutrients. While all fats should be consumed in moderation, there are good and bad fats. Good fats are what are known as unsaturated fats. They are found in olive oil, fatty fish like salmon, and nuts. Bad fats are saturated and trans fats. They are found in foods like butter, bacon, and ice cream. Consumption of foods that contain trans or saturated fats should be restricted or avoided altogether.

The main purpose of this passage is to

    A. Explain why fat is important for the body.
    B. Discuss some of the main sources of good fats.
    C. Talk about the different types of fats.
    D. Discuss examples of foods that should be avoided.

7. Satire is a genre that originated in the ancient world and is still popular today. Although satire is often humorous, its purposes and intentions go well beyond simply making people laugh. Satire is a way for the playwright, author, or television producer to criticize society, human nature, and individuals that he holds in contempt. Satire as we know it today developed in Ancient Greece and Rome. There were three main types. The first, Menippean satire, focused on criticizing aspects of human nature. This was done by introducing stereotypical, one-dimensional characters. Horatian satire can be viewed as gentle satire. It made fun of people and their habits, but in a way that was not offensive. Juvenalian satire was written is such a way that the audience would experience feelings of disgust and aversion when they saw the characters and their actions. Some of the most popular satires today are fake news shows, like the *Daily Show* and the *Colbert Report*, and satirical comic strips like *Doonesbury*.

The main purpose of the passage is

    A. To discuss the history of satire.
    B. To present the major types of satire.
    C. To discuss modern examples of satire.
    D. To present the purposes of satire.

8. Many people believe that how we express our feelings is mainly determined by our upbringing and culture. Undoubtedly, this is true in some cases. In North America, for example, it is customary to shake hands when we meet somebody to express acceptance, whereas in other countries they may simply bow slightly to indicate this. Many feelings, however, are expressed in similar ways by people all over the world. These emotions include, fear, anger, happiness, disgust, and sorrow. For example, if a person is experiencing fear, their eyes will widen and their pupils will dilate. This reaction is largely involuntary. The finding that people express many feelings in a similar manner, regardless of where they are from, indicates that facial expressions are influenced more by evolution than culture.

Based on the passage, it can be concluded that

    A. People often can't hide what they are feeling.
    B. People from other parts of the world express happiness differently.
    C. Fear is the only emotion that is felt by everybody in the world.
    D. Acceptance is a feeling invented by man.

9. Cities are typically warmer than the surrounding countryside, a phenomenon known as the heat island effect. There are numerous causes of this phenomenon, including emissions from cars and buildings. This creates a mini greenhouse effect. In rural areas, the standing water in marshes and ponds evaporates, which cools the air slightly. This does not occur to the same extent in the city. The tall buildings in the center of most cities block winds that would provide some relief from the excessive heat. Finally, the color and material of most roads and buildings absorbs rather than reflects heat. Although planting trees and using building materials that reflect heat may alleviate the problem somewhat, it will by no means eliminate it.

The main purpose of the passage is to

    A. Talk about how the problem of heat island can be solved.
    B. Argue that cities should make an effort to plant more trees.
    C. Present the major causes of the problem of heat island.
    D. Contrast the city environment to that of the countryside.

10. Marsupials resemble mammals in a number of ways. For one thing, they are warm-blooded creatures. They have hair, and the mothers feed their young by producing milk. However, one thing that separates marsupials from mammals is that their young are born when they are not yet fully-developed. Most are born after only about four or five weeks. They finish their development in the pouch of their mother. Some of the more commonly known marsupials are koalas, kangaroos, and opossums. They are a diverse group, with many members having little in common besides their reproductive traits.

A major difference between marsupials and mammals is

    A. Marsupials have hair, while mammals do not.
    B. Mammals are a much more diverse group than marsupials.
    C. Marsupials are born at an earlier stage of development.
    D. Mammals feed their young by producing milk.

Directions for questions 11–20

For the questions that follow, two sentences are followed by a question or statement. Read the sentences, then choose the best answer to the question or the best completion of the statement.

11. Atheists are individuals who do not believe in any type of higher power.

Theists usually possess religious and spiritual beliefs and have faith in one or more gods.

What does the second sentence do?

    A. It states an example.
    B. It makes a contrast.
    C. It disputes the first sentence.
    D. It offers a solution.

12. Home schooling refers to the practice of educating children at home rather than sending them to school.

Home schooling usually involves one parent giving up their career in order to stay home.

What does the second sentence do?

    A. It restates the information from the first.
    B. It provides an example.
    C. It states an effect.
    D. It contradicts the first.

13. Coffee is the most popular beverage in the entire world, and it is estimated that about 80% of Americans drink coffee.

According to a recent study, about 85% of North Americans drink soda, making it the most popular drink worldwide.

What does the second sentence do?

    A. It makes a contrast.
    B. It gives an example.
    C. It supports the first.
    D. It contradicts the first.

14. Regeneration refers to the ability that some animals have to replace severed body parts.

A salamander that has had its tail chopped off can grow a new one that is practically identical to the original.

What does the second sentence do?

    A. It restates the information from the first.
    B. It provides an example.
    C. It supports the first.
    D. It presents a solution.

15. Even though monthly rent on an apartment is usually less than a mortgage payment, most people would still rather own their own home.

Home ownership is a dream for most North Americans, even though monthly costs for houses are higher than those for apartments.

What does the second sentence do?

    A. It contradicts the first.
    B. It supports the first.
    C. It restates the information in the first.
    D. It explains the information in the first.

16. Soil contamination can be caused by a wide variety of factors, including leakage from underground septic tanks.

Septic tanks will corrode over time, and when they leak or rupture, the contents contaminate the surrounding soil.

What does the second sentence do?

    A. It expands on the first.
    B. It restates the information in the first.
    C. It states an effect.
    D. It proposes a solution.

17. The Richter Scale is the most commonly-used method to measure the strength of earthquakes.

Even though other methods are used more frequently to measure earthquakes, the Richter Scale is the most trusted.

What does the second sentence do?

    A. It provides an example.
    B. It reinforces the information in the first.
    C. It contradicts the information in the first.
    D. It presents a conclusion.

18. Adaptation refers to the ability of an animal to change in order to be better suited for its environment and to increase its chances of survival.

Porcupines have sharp quills that can be used to ward off animals that might otherwise try to hunt them.

What does the second sentence do?

    A. It expands on the information in the first.
    B. It presents an example.
    C. It states an effect.
    D. It makes an inference.

19. Congestion due to excessive traffic means that many people are forced to sit in traffic on their way to work.

Carpooling and public transportation can effectively reduce the number of cars on the road.
How are the two sentences related?

    A. They explain several concepts.
    B. They provide a concept and an example.
    C. They support one another.
    D. They state a problem and a solution.

20. Men are known for being analytical when they make decisions.

Women often make decisions based on intuition and gut feelings.

What does the second sentence do?

    A. It gives an example.
    B. It expands on the first.
    C. It provides a contrast.
    D. It contradicts the first.

Arithmetic

Solve the following problems and select your answer from the choices given. You may use the paper you have been given for scratch paper.

1. $6.42 - 3.7 =$
    A. 2.72
    B. 3.35
    C. 6.05
    D. 6.35

2. Which of the following fractions is equal to 0.375?
    A. $\frac{2}{5}$
    B. $\frac{2}{7}$
    C. $\frac{3}{8}$
    D. $\frac{4}{9}$

3. $5\frac{1}{6} - 2\frac{1}{2} =$
    A. $2\frac{1}{4}$
    B. $2\frac{2}{3}$
    C. $3\frac{1}{4}$
    D. $3\frac{1}{3}$

4. Which of the following is the best estimate for $23.97124 \div 8.023$?
    A. 2
    B. 3
    C. 16
    D. 20

5. The two legs of a right triangle have side lengths of 5 and 12. What is the length of the hypotenuse?
    A. 13
    B. 17
    C. $\sqrt{60}$
    D. $\sqrt{119}$

6. Which of the following fractions cannot be converted to a terminating decimal?
    A. $\frac{1}{2}$
    B. $\frac{1}{3}$
    C. $\frac{1}{4}$
    D. $\frac{1}{5}$

7. A dress is marked as 20% off. With the discount, the current price is $40.00. What is the price of the dress without the discount?

    A. $32

    B. $45

    C. $48

    D. $50

8. $17.92 \div 3.2 =$

    A. 5.1

    B. 5.6

    C. 6.1

    D. 6.6

9. Which of the following is *not* equal to the others?

    A. $\frac{10}{3}$

    B. $\frac{30}{9}$

    C. $2\frac{4}{3}$

    D. $3\frac{2}{3}$

10. If it takes Alice twelve minutes to make one ring, how many rings can she make in six hours?

    A. 2

    B. 6

    C. 30

    D. 72

11. Which of the following is closest to $\frac{111}{223} \cdot 5,940$?

    A. 1,000

    B. 2,000

    C. 3,000

    D. 4,000

12. $2.22 + 0.1 + 0.623 =$

    A. .855

    B. 8.46

    C. 2.853

    D. 2.943

13. Three treasure hunters decide to split up their haul. The first treasure hunter gets $\frac{1}{3}$ of the treasure. The second treasure hunter gets $\frac{1}{4}$ of the treasure. What fraction of the treasure does the third treasure hunter get?

    A. $\frac{1}{2}$

    B. $\frac{1}{5}$

    C. $\frac{5}{7}$

    D. $\frac{5}{12}$

14. What percentage is equal to $\frac{3}{20}$?

    A. 6%

    B. 15%

    C. 30%

    D. 60%

15. $1\frac{3}{4} \div \frac{7}{10} =$

    A. $2\frac{1}{2}$

    B. $2\frac{1}{14}$

    C. $1\frac{11}{14}$

    D. $\frac{4}{10}$

16. A rectangular lot is three yards wide and four yards long. What is the area of the lot in square feet?

    A. 4 ft²

    B. 12 ft²

    C. 36 ft²

    D. 108 ft²

17. $\frac{2}{3} + \frac{2}{5} =$

    A. $\frac{1}{4}$

    B. $\frac{1}{2}$

    C. $\frac{8}{15}$

    D. $1\frac{1}{15}$

Elementary Algebra

Solve the following problems and select your answer from the choices given. You may use the paper you have been given for scratch paper.

18. What is $|x| + |x - 2|$ when $x = 1$?

    A. 0

    B. 1

    C. 2

    D. 3

19. Which of the following inequalities is correct?

    A. $\frac{1}{3} < \frac{2}{7} < \frac{5}{12}$

    B. $\frac{2}{7} < \frac{1}{3} < \frac{5}{12}$

    C. $\frac{5}{12} < \frac{2}{7} < \frac{1}{3}$

    D. $\frac{5}{12} < \frac{1}{3} < \frac{2}{7}$

20. $\left(2x^2 + 3x + 2\right) - \left(x^2 + 2x - 3\right) =$

    A. $x^2 + x + 5$

    B. $x^2 + x - 1$

    C. $x^2 + 5x + 5$

    D. $x^2 + 5x - 1$

21. A rectangle is twice as long as it is wide. If its area is 200 cm², what is its width?

    A. 10 cm

    B. 20 cm

    C. $10\sqrt{2}$ cm

    D. $20\sqrt{2}$ cm

22. $\frac{\sqrt{2}}{\sqrt{6}} =$

    A. $\sqrt{3}$

    B. $2\sqrt{3}$

    C. $\frac{\sqrt{3}}{2}$

    D. $\frac{\sqrt{3}}{3}$

23. $\frac{2}{3}(3 - 2) + \frac{1}{2}(2 - 4) =$

    A. $-\frac{1}{3}$

    B. $-\frac{1}{2}$

    C. $\frac{1}{2}$

    D. $\frac{1}{3}$

24. Which of the following is *not* a factor of $x^3 - 3x^2 - 4x + 12$?

    A. $x - 2$
    B. $x + 2$
    C. $x - 3$
    D. $x + 3$

25. Simplify $\frac{x^6}{y^4} \cdot x^2 y^3$

    A. $x^4 y$
    B. $\frac{x^4}{y}$
    C. $x^8 y$
    D. $\frac{x^8}{y}$

26. If $6q + 3 = 8q - 7$, what is q?

    A. $-\frac{5}{7}$
    B. $\frac{5}{7}$
    C. 5
    D. -7

27. A communications company charges \$5.00 for the first ten minutes of a call and \$1.20 for each minute thereafter. Which of the following equations correctly relates the price in dollars, d, to the number of minutes, m (when $m \geq 10$)?

    A. $d = 5 + 1.2m$
    B. $d = 5 + 1.2(m - 10)$
    C. $d = 5m + 1.2(m + 10)$
    D. $d = (m + 10)(5 + 1.2)$

28. Which of the following graphs represents the inequality $-2 < x \leq 4$?

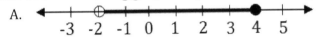

    A.

    B.

    C.

    D.

29. $(x + 2)(x - 3) = ?$

    A. $x^2 - 1$
    B. $x^2 - 6$
    C. $x^2 - x - 6$
    D. $x^2 - 5x - 1$

College Level Math

Solve the following problems and select your answer from the choices given. You may use the paper you have been given for scratch paper.

30. Which of the following completely describes the number of points in which two distinct quadratic functions can intersect?

    A. 2
    B. 0 or 1
    C. 0 or 2
    D. 1 or 2
    E. 0, 1, or 2

31. $\log_5(5^3) =$

    A. -2
    B. 1
    C. 3
    D. 25
    E. 243

32. Which of the following lines is perpendicular to the line $3x + 2y = 5$?

    A. $y = -\frac{1}{3}x + 2$
    B. $y = -\frac{2}{3}x + 5$
    C. $y = \frac{1}{3}x - 5$
    D. $y = \frac{2}{3}x - 7$
    E. $y = \frac{1}{3}x + 1$

33. If $\cos\theta + 1 = 0$, which of the following is a possible value of θ?

    A. $-180°$
    B. $-90°$
    C. $0°$
    D. $90°$
    E. $135°$

34. $(1 + i) \div (1 - i) =$

    A. i
    B. -1
    C. $-i$
    D. $-2i$
    E. $2i$

35. Suppose the area of the square in the diagram below is 64 in². (The square is not shown actual size.) What is the area of the circle?

A. 16π in²
B. 64π in²
C. $\frac{64}{\pi}$ in²
D. $(64 + \pi)$ in²
E. $\frac{128}{\pi}$ in²

36. How many solutions does the following system of equations have?
$$x^2 - y^2 = 2$$
$$x^2 + y^2 = 4$$

A. 0
B. 1
C. 2
D. 3
E. 4

37. If $f(x) = x^3 + 2$, what is $f^{-1}(x)$?
A. $x^{1/3} - 2$
B. $x^{-3} - 2$
C. $x^{-1/3} - 2$
D. $(x - 2)^{1/3}$
E. $(x - 2)^{-3}$

38. What is the period of the function $y = \tan(2x + 6)$?
A. $\frac{\pi}{2}$
B. π
C. 2π
D. 3π
E. 6π

39. One root of a certain real polynomial is $3 - 2i$. Which of the following must also be a root of this polynomial?
A. 0
B. $-2i$
C. $3 + 2i$
D. $-3 + 2i$
E. $2 - 3i$

40. What is the determinant of the matrix $\begin{bmatrix} 2 & 4 \\ 1 & 3 \end{bmatrix}$?

    A. -2
    B. -1
    C. 0
    D. 1
    E. 2

41. For one week, a hiker decides to walk two miles more each day than she walked the previous day. If she walks five miles on the first day, how many total miles has she walked by the end of the seventh day?

    A. 47
    B. 49
    C. 77
    D. 82
    E. 217

42. How many distinct ways are there to arrange the letters in the word PARABOLA?

    A. 1,680
    B. 6,720
    C 13,440
    D. 20,160
    E. 40,320

43. Which of the following points is collinear with the points $(2, 3)$ and $(-1, 5)$?

    A. $(-6, 8)$
    B. $(0, 4)$
    C. $(3, 2)$
    D. $(5, 1)$
    E. $(7, 0)$

44. Which of the following is equivalent to $x^2 + 3 > 2x + 2$?

    A. $x < -1$
    B. $x \neq 1$
    C. $x > 1$
    D. $-1 < x < 1$
    E. $x < -1$ or $x > 1$

45. A gardener has 300 feet of fencing. He wants to use it to enclose six identically-sized gardens, arranged as in the diagram below (not necessarily to scale). What is the maximum total area he can enclose? (Round to the nearest square foot if necessary.)

    A. 1600 ft^2
    B. 1667 ft^2
    C. 1869 ft^2
    D. 1875 ft^2
    E. 5625 ft^2

46. The points $(1, 2)$ and $(2, 4)$ lie on the graph of $f(x)$. Which of the following points must lie on the graph of $f^{-1}(x)$?

    A. $(1, 4)$
    B. $(2, 1)$
    C. $(2, 4)$
    D. $(2, -4)$
    E. $(4, 1)$

47. Which of the following could be the graph of $y = ax^7 - bx^4 + cx^2 - d$ for some positive constants a, b, c, and d? (Assume the graphs have no further maxima or minima beyond those shown.)

A. 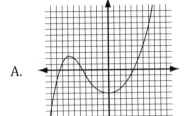 B. 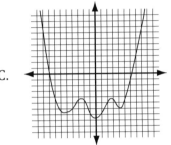 C.

D. 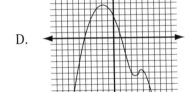 E.

48. If $f(x) = x + 3$ and $f(g(x)) = g(f(x))$, which of the following could be $g(x)$?

    A. $-x$
    B. $x - 4$
    C. $3x$
    D. x^2
    E. e^x

49. Which of the following expressions is equivalent to $\sin 2x \sec x$?

    A. 1
    B. $2 \sin x$
    C. $2 \cos x$
    D. $\sin^2 x$
    E. $\tan 2x$

Written Essay

Prepare an essay of about 300–600 words on the topic below.

Some people believe that everybody should vote in every election. They say that voting is an important democratic right that everybody should exercise whenever possible. Other people think that voting is not that important. They feel that if none of the candidates are offering anything that will benefit them, they are making a strong statement by not voting. Write an essay to someone who is deciding whether or not they should vote in the next election and take a position on whether you believe they should vote even if none of the candidates appeal to them. Use examples and arguments to support your position.

Answer Explanations

Sentence Skills

1. B: The phrase *to have extinction* in choice A is grammatically incorrect. In choice C, *causes* is plural, and so the word should be *exist* rather than *exists*. D is not the best choice because it is somewhat awkward. B sounds the best and is also grammatically correct.

2. C: C is the best answer because it indicates a contrast and is grammatically correct.

3. A: A is the best answer because it denotes the party to whom companies are offering tech support and because the verb *are* agrees with the noun *customers*.

4. D: D is the best choice. The phrases *high-fat diets* and *excessive amounts of television* agree with each other because they are both plural. The word *is* refers to *the fact that*, so these also agree with each other.

5. B: This is a well-known phrase meaning *despite what most people believe*. The word *contrarily* in choice A makes it incorrect. *Popularity* in choice C is out of place, and *believing* in choice D is incorrect.

6. A: B implies the Egyptians had long life spans, which doesn't make sense in the context of the sentence. C uses *its* instead of the grammatically correct *it's*, while D has misplaced commas and also uses *its*. A indicates the Egyptians lived a long time ago, and the correct form of *it's* is used.

7. B: The sentence describes a cause/effect relationship, so *because* is the correct way to begin the sentence. Choice A implies that technology changed in the past, which does not make sense in the context of the sentence. B indicates a cause/effect relationship, and states that technology is continuously changing, which is why IT professionals must continuously learn new skills.

8. D: D is the correct choice because the three verbs are in the same form. A and B use different verb forms. C is grammatically incorrect because of the *to* that is used to begin the sentence.

9. A: Saying that something can be *attributed to* something else is grammatically correct, which eliminates choices B and D. C is incorrect because *they* refers to antibiotics, so the sentence is essentially stating that antibiotics are prescribing. Inanimate objects are incapable of doing this, which makes the sentence incorrect. A states that antibiotics are prescribed, indicating someone else is doing the prescribing, which makes it the correct choice.

10. C: A is incorrect because *a* and *challenges* do not agree. B is incorrect because *key challenge* must be prefaced by *A* D is incorrect because of the misplaced apostrophe, and also because the sentence only identifies one challenge, meaning the plural, *key challenges*, is incorrect.

11. B: The original sentence states that serious complications can result if there are errors during the process of cell division. A and C refer to the process of cell division only, and not the errors that must be made for complications to occur. D indicates that the process leads to errors, rather than that the errors occur during the process.

12. A: The original sentence states that after much consideration a decision was made, which is why A is the best choice. The decision wasn't still difficult after much consideration, as B indicates, and she didn't immediately attend university, as is indicated by C. D simply doesn't make sense in the context of the statement.

13. A: A is the best choice because it is the only one that indicates a cause/effect relationship. Small business owners must do something *because* prices in department stores are too low for small business owners to match them.

14. A: The rewritten sentence begins with examples of some of the unique characteristics of ants. B does not indicate that they are unique characteristics; C describes them as fascinating rather than unique; and D does not make sense in the context of the sentence because of the phrase *of their* that follows *are unique characteristics*.

15. B: The word *despite* indicates that something is done in spite of warnings by law enforcement professionals, which eliminates choices C and D. A does not indicate precisely what motorists are failing to do, which eliminates that choice. B is the correct answer.

16. C: The original sentence states that many people believe the wolverine is related to wolves. They are related to weasels, but this is not something many people believe, eliminating choices A and D. The original sentence describes the strength of wolverines as a fact rather than a belief, eliminating choice B.

17. A: The word *because* indicates a cause/effect relationship. Since the phrase focuses on children, choice B can be eliminated. C does not indicate what "is of greater concern," so it can be eliminated. D is basically just describing the different types of ads, essentially restating something that has already been said. Answer choice A focuses on children and identifies advertising as the focus of the sentence, making it the best choice.

18. C: C is the only choice that offers an explanation as to why people have accumulated debt. A and D cannot logically follow the introductory phrase. B was not a fact expressed in the original sentence.

19. B: A indicates shipping costs can be charged because consumers are not saving as much money as they think, which is not an idea expressed in the original sentence. C states they may not be saving as much money as they think because they can find low prices, an idea that is also not stated in the original sentence. D indicates that companies shop online, an idea not expressed in the original sentence. B indicates there is a reason why people are not saving as much as they think. It then identifies people and companies, which are also identified in the original sentence, making it the correct choice.

20. D: A is too general, indicating that an individual will always profit if a company's stock decreases. B indicates that the right to sell shares is contingent on the decrease of a company's stock, which is also not the case. C indicates the individual will profit from a decrease or an increase, but the original sentence clearly states there will be no profit if a stock increases. D tells how an individual can profit if the value of a stock decreases (by purchasing a put), making it the correct choice.

Reading Comprehension

1. B: In describing the marketing of "sea monkeys," the author describes it as creative genius, and attributes their popularity to the drawings and advertisements that appeared in comic books. It is reasonable to conclude that without the branding and (somewhat misleading) ads, they wouldn't have been as popular. Marketing them under the less exciting brand name "brine shrimp" likely wouldn't have resulted in as many sales.

2. C: A is incorrect because the passage states they were similar in size. The cost of production is not mentioned, eliminating B as a possibility. D is incorrect because it was the eight-track tape that was included in these vehicles. C is correct because the passage states the eight-track tape could store and play twice as many songs.

3. B: The passage states that, "Often, the agoraphobic will view his home as the safest possible place to be, and he may even be reluctant to leave his house," making B the correct choice.

4. D: B and C are only briefly mentioned, allowing them to be eliminated as possibilities. Although the passage does discuss what could happen to two balls released at the top of a mountain, that is not the purpose of the passage, so A can be eliminated. The purpose is to show how small differences (in this case two inches between two rubber balls) can have large effects. This is essentially what the butterfly effect is, and the purpose of the passage is to give an example to demonstrate this principle.

5. A: The passage discusses several problems that can occur with wells. Both of the problems mentioned are associated with wells that are too shallow; no problems associated with wells that are too deep are mentioned. Therefore, it seems safe to conclude that a deeper well would be more desirable than a shallow one.

6. C: A is mentioned only briefly in the passage. B and D are mentioned, but this information does not fit into the overall purpose of the passage, which is to discuss the different types of fats, both good and bad.

7. B: C and D are mentioned only briefly. Although the history of satire is discussed, most of the passage focuses on discussing the three major forms of satire that originated in Ancient Greece and Rome, making B the best choice.

8. A: B is incorrect because the passage states that happiness is expressed similarly by people all over the world. C is incorrect because the passage states that there are many emotions felt and expressed by people all over the world. D is incorrect because, although people may express acceptance differently, that is not sufficient to conclude it is not a natural emotion. A is correct. We can conclude that people can't always hide what they are feeling because of the statement in the passage that the facial expressions associated with emotions like fear are largely involuntary.

9. C: C is the correct answer because the passage mainly focuses on discussing the causes of heat island. A, B, and D are touched upon only in passing.

10. C: A and D are incorrect because the passage states that these are characteristics that marsupials and mammals share. B can be eliminated, because it is not mentioned in the passage. C is the correct choice, as "one thing that separates marsupials from mammals is that their young are born when they are not yet fully-developed" is stated in the passage.

11. B: Theists are the opposite of atheists, so the second sentence provides a contrast to the first.

12. C: The first sentence introduces the concept of home schooling. The second sentence states that one parent usually has to give up their job for home schooling to take place, which is a direct effect of the practice of home schooling.

13. D: The first sentence states that coffee is the most popular beverage. The second sentence directly contradicts it, stating that soda is the most popular. The second sentence contradicts the first.

14. B: A salamander's ability to grow a new tail is an example of the ability to replace severed body parts, which is known as regeneration. The second sentence provides an example of the concept explained in the first.

15. C: Both sentences give the same information, and nothing new is added. The second sentence restates the information from the first.

16. A: The second sentence tells how septic tanks can contribute to the problem of soil contamination. Both contamination and septic tanks are mentioned in the first sentence. Therefore, the second sentence expands on the first.

17. C: The first sentence states that the Richter Scale is the most commonly-used method to measure the strength of earthquakes. The second sentence states that other methods are used more frequently. Therefore, the second sentence contradicts the information in the first.

18. B: The first sentence introduces the concept of adaptation, which refers to an animal's ability to change in order to increase its chances of survival. A porcupine's quills allow it to defend itself against potential predators, thereby increasing its chances of survival. The second sentence provides an example of the concept presented in the first.

19. D: The first sentence states a problem: congestion due to excessive traffic. The second sentence offers a solution: carpooling can reduce the amount of traffic on roads, which could logically help ease congestion.

20. C: The first sentence describes how men make decisions. The second sentence describes the different process that is used by women to make decisions, which provides a contrast to the first.

Arithmetic

1. A: In order to subtract decimal numbers, write them one above the other with the decimal points aligned; then, carry out the subtraction normally, placing the decimal point in the same position in the result:

$$\begin{array}{r} 6.42 \\ -\ 3.24 \\ \hline 2.72 \end{array}$$

2. C: 0.375 is *three hundred seventy-five thousandths*, which, when written as a fraction, is $\frac{375}{1000}$. One way this fraction can be reduced by dividing both the numerator and denominator repeatedly by 5: $\frac{375}{1000} = \frac{75}{200} = \frac{15}{40} = \frac{3}{8}$.

3. B: One way to add or subtract mixed numbers is to first convert them to improper fractions. To get the numerator of the improper fraction, multiply the integer part of the mixed number by the denominator and add that product to the numerator; the denominator remains the same. So $5\frac{1}{6} = \frac{5 \times 6 + 1}{6} = \frac{31}{6}$ and $2\frac{1}{2} = \frac{2 \times 2 + 1}{2} = \frac{5}{2}$. Now convert the improper fractions to so that they have the lowest common denominator, which in this case is 6. $\frac{31}{6}$ already has a denominator of 6, but we need to

119

convert $\frac{5}{2}$ to its equivalent fraction with a denominator of 6: $\frac{5}{2} = \frac{5 \times 3}{2 \times 3} = \frac{15}{6}$. We can now subtract. $\frac{31}{6} - \frac{15}{6} = \frac{16}{6}$, which we can reduce by dividing both sides by 2 to $\frac{16/2}{6/2} = \frac{8}{3}$. Finally, we convert back to a mixed number by dividing the numerator by the denominator; the quotient is the integer part, and the remainder is the new numerator. $8 \div 3 = 2$ with a remainder of 2, so $\frac{8}{3} = 2\frac{2}{3}$.

4. B: 23.97124 is about 24, and 8.023 is about 8. So $23.97124 \div 8.023$ is about $24 \div 8 = 3$.

5. A: The legs and hypotenuse of a right triangle are related through the Pythagorean Theorem, $a^2 + b^2 = c^2$, where a and b are the lengths of the legs and c is the length of the hypotenuse. In this case, $a = 5$ and $b = 12$ (or vice-versa; it doesn't matter which leg we call a and which leg we call b), so $5^2 + 12^2 = c^2$; $25 + 144 = c^2$; $169 = c^2$; $c = \sqrt{169} = 13$.

6. B: A terminating decimal is one that eventually stops; after a certain place all further digits are zeroes. To convert a fraction to a decimal, divide the numerator by the denominator. This quickly produces terminating decimals for $\frac{1}{2}, \frac{1}{4}$, and $\frac{1}{5}$, namely 0.5, 0.25, and 0.2, respectively. The decimal expansion of $\frac{1}{3}$, however, repeats indefinitely as 0.33333333... Alternately, note that in order to correspond to a terminating decimal, a fraction must have a denominator that is a factor of a power of ten; in other words, the only prime factors of the denominator must be 2 and 5. This is true of $\frac{1}{2}, \frac{1}{4}$, and $\frac{1}{5}$ but not of $\frac{1}{3}$. So, $\frac{1}{3}$ is the only one of the choices without a terminating decimal expansion.

7. D: If the dress's price is 20% off, it is (100% – 20%) = 80% of the regular price. So, the sales price of the dress, \$40, is 80% of what price? To find the answer, divide 40 by 80%, which is equivalent to the fraction $\frac{80}{100}$. Dividing by the fraction $\frac{80}{100}$ is the same as multiplying its reciprocal, $\frac{100}{80}$. $40 \times \frac{100}{80} = 40 \times \frac{5}{4} = \frac{200}{4} = 50$, so the original price was \$50.00.

8. B: To divide decimals, set up a long division problem, but then move the decimal point to the right in both the dividend *and* the divisor until it is at the right end of the divisor, making the divisor an integer. Then, put the decimal point in the quotient directly above the decimal point in the dividend. Add extra zeroes to the end of the dividend if needed.

$$3.2 \overline{)17.92} = 32 \overline{)179.2}$$

with quotient 5.6:

$$
\begin{array}{r}
5.6 \\
32\overline{)179.2} \\
\underline{160} \\
192 \\
\underline{192} \\
0
\end{array}
$$

9. D: Multiplying both the numerator and denominator by the same constant does not change the value of a fraction; for instance, $\frac{10}{3} = \frac{10 \times 3}{3 \times 3} = \frac{30}{9}$, so choices A and B contain equivalent fractions. To convert a mixed number to a fraction, multiply the integer part by the denominator and add the product it to the numerator; this becomes the numerator of the improper fraction, while the denominator remains the same. So, $2\frac{4}{3} = \frac{2 \times 3 + 4}{3} = \frac{10}{3}$. (Note that $2\frac{4}{3}$ is a nonstandard mixed number because it has an improper fractional component; nevertheless, it is equivalent to $\frac{10}{3}$ and $\frac{30}{9}$.)

Though choices A, B, and C are equal to each other, choice D contains a nonequivalent mixed number: $3\frac{2}{3} = \frac{3\times3+2}{3} = \frac{11}{3} \neq \frac{10}{3}$. (As a standard mixed number, $\frac{10}{3}$ would be equal to $3\frac{1}{3}$.)

10. C: Six hours is equal to $6 \times 60 = 360$ minutes. If Alice can create one ring in twelve minutes, then in 360 minutes she can create $\frac{360}{12} = 30$ rings.

Here is another way to solve the problem. A rate of one ring in twelve minutes is equivalent to a rate of $\frac{1 \text{ ring}}{12 \text{ minutes}} \times \frac{60 \text{ minutes}}{1 \text{ hour}} = \frac{5 \text{ rings}}{\text{hour}}$. Therefore, in six hours Alice can create $5 \times 6 = 30$ rings.

11. C: $\frac{111}{223}$ is very close to $\frac{1}{2}$. 5,940 is close to 6,000. So $\frac{111}{223} \times 5{,}940$ is about $\frac{1}{2} \times 6{,}000 = 3{,}000$.

12. D: In order to add decimal numbers, write them one above the other with the decimal points aligned, and then carry out the addition normally, placing the decimal point in the same position in the result:

```
   2.22
 + 0.1
 + 0.623
   2.943
```

13. D: The total must be 1, so the fraction that goes to the third treasure hunter is $1 - \frac{1}{3} - \frac{1}{4}$. To subtract these fractions, convert them all to fractions with the least common denominator, which is in this case 12. So $1 - \frac{1}{3} - \frac{1}{4} = \frac{1\times12}{1\times12} - \frac{1\times4}{3\times4} - \frac{1\times3}{4\times3} = \frac{12}{12} - \frac{4}{12} - \frac{3}{12} = \frac{12-4-3}{12} = \frac{5}{12}$.

14. B: A percentage is the numerator of a fraction with a denominator of 100. To convert a fraction to a percentage, determine by what number the denominator must be multiplied so that it is 100, and multiply the numerator and denominator by that number. $\frac{100}{20} = 5$, so $\frac{3}{20} = \frac{3\times5}{20\times5} = \frac{15}{100}$. Therefore, $\frac{3}{20} = 15\%$.

15. A: To multiply or divide mixed numbers, first convert them to improper fractions. To get the numerator of the equivalent improper fraction, multiply the denominator of the mixed number's fractional component by the whole number component and add to the numerator of the fractional component; keep the denominator of the improper fraction the same as the denominator of the fractional component of the mixed number. So $1\frac{3}{4} = \frac{1\times4+3}{4} = \frac{7}{4}$. Dividing by a fraction is the same as multiplying by its reciprocal, so $\frac{7}{4} \div \frac{7}{10} = \frac{7}{4} \times \frac{10}{7} = \frac{70}{28}$, which reduces to $\frac{70\div7}{28\div7} = \frac{10}{4} = \frac{10\div2}{4\div2} = \frac{5}{2}$. Convert this back to a mixed number by dividing the numerator by the denominator: the quotient is the integer part of the mixed number, and the remainder is the numerator of the fractional part of the mixed number. $5 \div 2 = 2$ with a remainder of 1, so $\frac{5}{2} = 2\frac{1}{2}$.

16. D: There are three feet in a yard. In feet, the lot is $3 \times 3 = 9$ feet wide, and $4 \times 3 = 12$ feet long. So its area is $9 \text{ ft} \times 12 \text{ ft} = 108$ square feet.

As an alternate way of solving the problem, first find the lot's area in square yards: 3 yards $\times$ 4 yards $= 12$ square yards. Then, convert square yards to square feet: since there are 3 feet in a yard, there are $3^2 = 9$ square feet in a square yard. So the lot's area in square feet is $12 \times 9 = 108$ square feet.

17. D: To add or subtract fractions, first convert them to equivalent fractions which contain the lowest common denominator, which in this case is 15. So $\frac{2}{3} + \frac{2}{5} = \frac{2\times5}{3\times5} + \frac{2\times3}{5\times3} = \frac{10}{15} + \frac{6}{15} = \frac{16}{15}$. To convert this to a mixed number, divide the numerator by the denominator; the quotient is the integer part of the mixed number and the remainder is the numerator of the fractional part of the mixed number. $16 \div 15 = 1$ with a remainder of 1, so $\frac{16}{15} = 1\frac{1}{15}$.

Elementary Algebra

18. C: $|x| + |x - 2| = |1| + |1 - 2| = |1| + |-1| = 1 + 1 = 2$.

19. B: One way to compare fractions is to convert them to equivalent fractions which have common denominators. In this case the lowest common denominator of the three fractions is $7 \times 12 = 84$. Converting each of the fractions to this denominator, $\frac{1}{3} = \frac{1\times28}{3\times28} = \frac{28}{84}$, $\frac{2}{7} = \frac{2\times12}{7\times12} = \frac{24}{84}$, and $\frac{5}{12} = \frac{5\times7}{12\times7} = \frac{35}{84}$. Since $24 < 28 < 35$, it must be the case that $\frac{2}{7} < \frac{1}{3} < \frac{5}{12}$.

20. A: $(2x^2 + 3x + 2) - (x^2 + 2x - 3) = (2x^2 + 3x + 2) + (-1)(x^2 + 2x - 3)$. First, distribute the -1 to remove the parentheses: $2x^2 + 3x + 2 - x^2 - 2x + 3$. Next, combine like terms: $(2x^2 - x^2) + (3x - 2x) + (2 + 3) = x^2 + x + 5$.

21. A: The area A of a rectangle is equal to its length l times its width w: $A = l \times w$. The rectangle is twice as long as it is wide, so $l = 2w$. By replacing l with its equivalent $2w$, the area of this rectangle can be written as $A = 2w \times w = 2w^2$. So $2w^2 = 200$ cm^2; $w^2 = 100$ cm^2; $w = \sqrt{100 \text{ cm}^2} = 10$ cm.

22. D: To rationalize the denominator of a ratio of radicals, multiply both sides of the fraction by the radical in the denominator and reduce if necessary: $\frac{\sqrt{2}}{\sqrt{6}} = \frac{\sqrt{2}\times\sqrt{6}}{\sqrt{6}\times\sqrt{6}} = \frac{\sqrt{12}}{6} = \frac{2\sqrt{3}}{6} = \frac{\sqrt{3}}{3}$.

23. A: $\frac{2}{3}(3 - 2) + \frac{1}{2}(2 - 4) = \frac{2}{3}(1) + \frac{1}{2}(-2) = \frac{2}{3} - \frac{2}{2} = \frac{2}{3} - 1 = \frac{2}{3} - \frac{3}{3} = -\frac{1}{3}$.

24. D: Note that the first two terms and the last two terms of $x^3 - 3x^2 - 4x + 12$ are each divisible by $x - 3$. Thus $x^3 - 3x^2 - 4x + 12 = x^2(x - 3) - 4(x - 3) = (x^2 - 4)(x - 3)$. $x^2 - 4$ is a difference of squares, and since in general $x^2 - a^2 = (x + a)(x - a)$, we know $x^2 - 4 = (x + 2)(x - 2)$. The full factorization of $x^3 - 3x^2 - 4x + 12$ is therefore $(x + 2)(x - 2)(x - 3)$.

Alternatively, instead of factoring the polynomial, we could have divided the polynomial $x^3 - 3x^2 - 4x + 12$ by the expression contained in each answer choice. Of those listed, only the expression x+3 yields a nonzero remainder when divided into $x^3 - 3x^2 - 4x + 12$, so it is not a factor.

25. D: $\frac{x^6}{y^4} \times x^2y^3 = x^6y^{-4} \times x^2y^3 = (x^6x^2)(y^{-4}y^3) = x^{6+2}y^{-4+3} = x^8y^{-1} = \frac{x^8}{y}$.

26. C: $6q + 3 = 8q - 7 \Rightarrow 6q + 3 + 7 = 8q \Rightarrow 6q + 10 = 8q \Rightarrow 10 = 8q - 6q \Rightarrow 10 = 2q \Rightarrow q = 5$.

27. B: The charge is $1.20 for each minute *past* the first ten minutes. The number of minutes after the first ten minutes is $m - 10$, so this amount charged for the part of the phone call exceeding 10 minutes is $1.2(m - 10)$. Adding this to the $5.00 charge for the first ten minutes gives $d = 5 + 1.2(m - 10)$.

28. A: When graphing an inequality, a solid circle at an endpoint means that the number at that endpoint is included in the range, while a hollow circle means it is not. Since the inequality says that *x* is strictly greater than 2, the circle at 2 should therefore be hollow; since the inequality says that *x* is less than *or equal to* 4, the circle at 4 should be solid. $2 < x \leq 4$ indicates that *x* is between 2 and 4, so the area between the circles should be shaded; the two end rays in choice D would instead represent the pair of inequalities "$x < 2$ or $x \geq 4$".

29. C: A method commonly taught to multiply binomials is the "FOIL" method, an acronym for First, Outer, Inner, Last: multiply the first terms of each factor, then the outer terms, and so forth. Applied to $(x + 2)(x - 3)$, this yields $(x)(x) + (x)(-3) + (2)(x) + (2)(-3) = x^2 - 3x + 2x - 6 = x^2 - x - 6$.

College Level Math

30. E: It is certainly possible for two distinct quadratic functions to intersect at no points; one simple example is provided by the quadratic functions $y = x^2$ and $y = x^2 + 1$. For these to have an intersection would require a solution to the equation $x^2 = x^2 + 1$, which implies $0 = 1$, which is clearly impossible. It is also possible for two quadratic functions to intersect in exactly one point, if that point is the vertex of both quadratic functions; take for instance the quadratic functions $y = x^2$ and $y = -x^2$, which intersect only at the origin, $(0, 0)$. Two distinct quadratic functions intersecting at a point other than a mutual vertex will intersect at two points; an example is the quadratic functions $y = x^2$ and $y = -x^2 + 2$, which will intersect at the points $(1,1)$ and $(-1,1)$.

31. C: For any base b, $\log_b x$ and b^x are inverse functions, so $\log_b(b^x) = b^{\log_b x} = x$. In particular, then, $\log_5(5^3) = 3$.

32. D: Perpendicular lines have opposite inverse slopes. The four answer choices are all in slope-intercept form, in which the slope is simply the coefficient of *x*; the slopes of the lines in the choices are, respectively, $-\frac{1}{3}, -\frac{2}{3}, \frac{1}{3}, \frac{2}{3}$, and $\frac{1}{3}$. The given line, $3x + 2y = 5$, is *not* in slope-intercept form but in standard form; to find its slope, we can convert the equation to slope-intercept form and determine the coefficient of x: $3x + 2y = 5 \Rightarrow 2y = -3x + 5 \Rightarrow y = -\frac{3}{2}x + \frac{5}{2}$. The slope of this line is $-\frac{3}{2}$. Its negative reciprocal is $-\left(-\frac{3}{2}\right)^{-1} = -\left(-\frac{2}{3}\right) = \frac{2}{3}$. This matches the slope of the line in choice D, which is therefore perpendicular to the given line.

33. A: If $\cos\theta + 1 = 0$, then $\cos\theta = -1$. This has only one solution in the interval $0° \leq \theta < 360°$, namely $\theta = 180°$. This is not one of the answer choices; however, the cosine function has a period of 360°, which means that adding or subtracting any multiple of 360° to the argument does not change the result. Since $180° - 360° = -180°$, $\cos(-180°) = \cos(180°) = -1$, so $-180°$ is also a solution to the equation.

34. A: To divide complex numbers, write the quotient as a fraction, and then simplify it by multiplying both the numerator and denominator by the complex conjugate of the denominator. (The complex conjugate of $a + bi$ is defined as $a - bi$.) This guarantees that the new denominator will be a positive real number. So, $(1 + i) \div (1 - i) = \frac{(1+i)(1+i)}{(1-i)(1+i)} = \frac{1+i+i+i^2}{1+i-i-i^2} = \frac{1+2i+i^2}{1-i^2}$. Since $i^2 = -1$, this becomes $\frac{1+2i+(-1)}{1-(-1)} = \frac{2i}{2} = i$.

35. A: The area of a square is equal to the square of the length of one side. If the area is 64 in², the side length must therefore be $\sqrt{64\text{in}^2} = 8$ in. The circle is inscribed in the square, so the side length of the square is the same as the circle's diameter. If the circle's diameter is 8 in, then the circle's radius must be half of that, or 4 in. The area of a circle is equal to $A = \pi r^2 = \pi(4 \text{ in})^2 = 16\pi \text{ in}^2$.

36. E: The given pair of equations can be solved as a linear system of two variables, x^2 and y^2. This system can be solved by a number of methods; for instance, we can solve the first equation for x^2 to get $x^2 = y^2 + 2$ and then substitute that in to the second equation to get $(y^2 + 2) + y^2 = 4$, which simplifies to $2y^2 = 2$, or $y^2 = 1$. Substituting 1 for y^2 into $x^2 = y^2 + 2$ gives $x^2 = 1 + 2 = 3$. This gives a unique solution for x^2 and y^2, but not for x and y, since each of these can be positive or negative: if $x^2 = 3$, then $x = \pm\sqrt{3}$, and if $y^2 = 1$, then $y = \pm 1$. There are therefore four solutions in all: $x = \sqrt{3}, y = 1$; $x = -\sqrt{3}, y = 1$; $x = \sqrt{3}, y = -1$; or $x = -\sqrt{3}, y = -1$. (Note that it would have been possible to come to this conclusion about the number of solutions without actually finding the solutions.)

As an alternate method of solving the problem, note that the first equation describes a hyperbola and the second a circle, both centered at the origin. A graph of both functions shows that they intersect in four points, one in each quadrant.

37. D: $f^{-1}(x)$ signifies the *inverse function* of $f(x)$, the function such that $f(f^{-1}(x)) = f^{-1}(f(x)) = x$. Though we could try compositing each function given in the answer choices with the original $f(x)$ to see which composition simplified to x, there are more straightforward ways of finding inverse functions. Replacing $f(x)$ in the original equation with x, and replace x in the original equation with x $f^{-1}(x)$. Thus, $= (f^{-1}(x))^3 + 2$. Now, simply solve for $f^{-1}(x)$. We can first subtract 2 from both sides, to yield $x - 2 = (f^{-1}(x))^3$, and then take the cube root of both sides (i.e. raise both sides to the power of $\frac{1}{3}$) to get $(x - 2)^{\frac{1}{3}} = f^{-1}(x)$.

38. A: The period of the unmodified tangent function $y = \tan(x)$ is simply π. However, when the x is multiplied by a coefficient $b \neq 1$, the function is compressed or stretched horizontally, changing its period to $\frac{\pi}{|b|}$. Here, $b = 2$, so the new period is $\frac{\pi}{2}$. (The "+6" in the given equation shifts the function horizontally but has no effect on the period.)

39. C: A real polynomial is a polynomial in which all of the coefficients are real numbers. ($3x^2 + 2x - 5$ is a real polynomial; $2x^2 + ix - 3$ is not since one of the coefficients, i, is imaginary.) It is possible for a real polynomial to have complex roots; however, if a complex number is a root of a real polynomial, then its complex conjugate must also be a root of that polynomial. (The complex conjugate of $a + bi$ is defined as $a - bi$.) Therefore, if $3 - 2i$ is a root of a real polynomial, so must be its complex conjugate, $3 + 2i$.

40. E: The determinant of a 2×2 matrix $\begin{bmatrix} a & b \\ c & d \end{bmatrix}$ is $\begin{vmatrix} a & b \\ c & d \end{vmatrix} = ad - bc$. Plugging in the values of the given matrix gives $2 \times 3 - 4 \times 1 = 6 - 4 = 2$.

41. C: If the hiker walks two miles more each day than she walked the previous day, then the distances she walks on successive days make up an arithmetic sequence, with a common difference of 2. (The definition of an arithmetic sequence is that the difference between two adjacent terms is constant; since the difference between the distances the hiker walks on any two consecutive days is 2, this condition is satisfied.) The formula for the nth term of an arithmetic sequence is $a_n = a_1 + (n - 1)d$, where a_1 is the first term and d is the common difference, and the sum of the first n terms of an arithmetic series is $S_n = \frac{n}{2}(a_1 + a_n)$. Here the distance the hiker walks on the seventh day is $a_7 = a_1 + (7 - 1)d = 5 + (6)(2) = 17$, and so the total distance she walks in all seven days is $S_7 = \frac{7}{2}(a_1 + a_7) = \frac{7}{2}(5 + 17) = \frac{7}{2}(22) = 77$.

42. B: In general, the number of ways to arrange 8 items is simply 8! = 40,320. However, PARABOLA has three As; two arrangements of the letters of PARABOLA that differ only in changing the As around are not distinct words. Since the As can be ordered in 3! = 6 ways, the general calculation of 8! counts each distinct arrangement of letters 6 times. So, to find the number of *distinct* arrangements of the letters in PARABOLA, it is necessary to divide: $\frac{8!}{3!} = \frac{40,320}{6} = 6,720$ (or, using the properties of factorials to simplify the calculation, $\frac{8!}{3!} = 8 \times 7 \times 6 \times 5 \times 4 = 6,720$).

43. D: "Collinear" means the points lie along the same line. There are several ways to solve this problem; one is to find the equation of the line that passes through the two given points and see which of the points in the answer choices fits the equation. The slope of the line passing through the points $(2, 3)$ and $(-1, 5)$ is $= \frac{y_2 - y_1}{x_2 - x_1} = \frac{5-3}{-1-2} = -\frac{2}{3}$. The equation of the line is therefore $y = -\frac{2}{3}x + b$ for some constant b. To find b, substitute either of the original points as x and y; using $(2, 3)$, we get $3 = -\frac{2}{3}(2) + b \Rightarrow 3 = -\frac{4}{3} + b \Rightarrow b = 3 + \frac{4}{3} = \frac{9}{3} + \frac{4}{3} = \frac{13}{3}$. So the equation of the line is $y = -\frac{2}{3}x + \frac{13}{3}$. If we put in the coordinates of the four given points, the only one that satisfies the equation is D, $(5,1)$: $-\frac{2}{3}(5) + \frac{13}{3} = -\frac{10}{3} + \frac{13}{3} = \frac{3}{3} = 1$.

44. B: To simplify the given inequality, first move all the terms to one side: $x^2 + 3 > 2x + 2 \Rightarrow x^2 + 3 - 2x - 2 > 0 \Rightarrow x^2 - 2x + 1 > 0$. Now, factor the left-hand side: $x^2 - 2x + 1 = (x - 1)(x - 1) = (x - 1)^2$. The original inequality is equivalent to $(x - 1)^2 > 0$. Since the square of a negative number is positive, $(x - 1)^2 > 0$ everywhere except where $x - 1 = 0$, i.e. at $x = 1$.

45. D: Call the total width of the enclosed plot x and the length y. Then the area enclosed is $A = xy$. We can reduce this to a function of one variable by using other information. Note from the diagram that there are four stretches of fencing spanning the full width and three spanning the length, so the total amount of fencing used is $4x + 3y$. Since the gardener has 300 feet of fencing, $4x + 3y = 300$. Solving for y yields $y = -\frac{4}{3}x + 100$. Substitute $-\frac{4}{3}x + 100$ into the area equation: $A = x\left(-\frac{4}{3}x + 100\right) = -\frac{4}{3}x^2 + 100x$. This is the equation of a parabola opening downward, so the maximum value of the area occurs at the parabola's vertex. We can find the coordinates of the vertex of the parabola, (h, k), by completing the square to put the area equation in standard form, $A = (x - h)^2 + k$, but a faster method is to simply use the equation for the x-coordinate of the vertex, $h = -\frac{b}{2a}$ (where a and b are respectively the coefficients of x^2 and of x). So $h = -\frac{100}{2\left(\frac{4}{3}\right)} = -\frac{100}{\frac{8}{3}} = -\frac{300}{8} = -37.5$. So, the area is at a maximum when $x = 37.5$. Putting this into the area equation $A = x\left(-\frac{4}{3}x + 100\right)$ yields $A = 37.5\left(-\frac{4}{3}(37.5) + 100\right) = 37.5(-50 + 100) = (37.5)(50) = 1,875$ square feet.

46. B: If the point (a, b) lies on the graph of $f(x)$, then $f(a) = b$. If $f(a) = b$, then $f^{-1}(b) = a$. Therefore, if the point (a, b) lies on the graph of $f(x)$, the point (b, a) must lie on the graph of $f^{-1}(x)$. So since $(1,2)$ lies on the graph of $f(x)$, $(2,1)$ must lie on the graph of $f^{-1}(x)$.

47. A: Consider the end behavior of the polynomial, which is entirely determined by its highest-order term, the term with the largest exponent. If the exponent is odd and the coefficient positive, then the graph goes down on the left and up on the right; if the exponent is odd and the coefficient is negative, the graph goes up on the left and down on the. If the exponent is even and the coefficient is positive, then the graph goes up on both sides; if the exponent is even and the coefficient is negative, the graph goes down on both sides. Here the highest-order term is ax^7; we are told that all the coefficients are positive, so the term has an odd exponent and a positive coefficient. This means it must go down on the left and up on the right, and the only graph among the answer choices that does this is A. (Choice E doesn't go down on either side, but instead tends toward a horizontal asymptote; this cannot occur for a polynomial, though it's possible for a rational function.)

48. B: If $f(x) = x + 3$, then $f(g(x)) = g(x) + 3$ and $g(f(x)) = g(x + 3)$. We are asked for which of these possibilities of $g(x)$ is it true that $g(x) + 3 = g(x + 3)$. The only one for which this is true is B, $g(x) = x - 4$: $g(x) + 3 = (x - 4) + 3 = x - 1$, and $g(x + 3) = (x + 3) - 4 = x - 1$. $x - 1 = x - 1$, so the condition is satisfied. In contrast if we try, for example, choice A, $g(x) = -x$, we get $g(x) + 3 = (-x) + 3 = -x + 3$, and $g(x + 3) = -(x + 3) = -x - 3$; $-x + 3 \neq -x - 3$, so this does not satisfy the condition of the problem.

49. B: The most straightforward way of solving this problem is to take advantage of the double-angle formula, $\sin 2x = 2 \sin x \cos x$. $\sin 2x \sec x = 2 \sin x \cos x \sec x = 2 \sin x \cos x \left(\frac{1}{\cos x}\right) = 2 \sin x$.

How to Overcome Test Anxiety

Just the thought of taking a test is enough to make most people a little nervous. A test is an important event that can have a long-term impact on your future, so it's important to take it seriously and it's natural to feel anxious about performing well. But just because anxiety is normal, that doesn't mean that it's helpful in test taking, or that you should simply accept it as part of your life. Anxiety can have a variety of effects. These effects can be mild, like making you feel slightly nervous, or severe, like blocking your ability to focus or remember even a simple detail.

If you experience test anxiety—whether severe or mild—it's important to know how to beat it. To discover this, first you need to understand what causes test anxiety.

Causes of Test Anxiety

While we often think of anxiety as an uncontrollable emotional state, it can actually be caused by simple, practical things. One of the most common causes of test anxiety is that a person does not feel adequately prepared for their test. This feeling can be the result of many different issues such as poor study habits or lack of organization, but the most common culprit is time management. Starting to study too late, failing to organize your study time to cover all of the material, or being distracted while you study will mean that you're not well prepared for the test. This may lead to cramming the night before, which will cause you to be physically and mentally exhausted for the test. Poor time management also contributes to feelings of stress, fear, and hopelessness as you realize you are not well prepared but don't know what to do about it.

Other times, test anxiety is not related to your preparation for the test but comes from unresolved fear. This may be a past failure on a test, or poor performance on tests in general. It may come from comparing yourself to others who seem to be performing better or from the stress of living up to expectations. Anxiety may be driven by fears of the future—how failure on this test would affect your educational and career goals. These fears are often completely irrational, but they can still negatively impact your test performance.

> **Review Video: 3 Reasons You Have Test Anxiety**
> Visit mometrix.com/academy and enter code: 428468

127

Elements of Test Anxiety

As mentioned earlier, test anxiety is considered to be an emotional state, but it has physical and mental components as well. Sometimes you may not even realize that you are suffering from test anxiety until you notice the physical symptoms. These can include trembling hands, rapid heartbeat, sweating, nausea, and tense muscles. Extreme anxiety may lead to fainting or vomiting. Obviously, any of these symptoms can have a negative impact on testing. It is important to recognize them as soon as they begin to occur so that you can address the problem before it damages your performance.

Review Video: 3 Ways to Tell You Have Test Anxiety
Visit mometrix.com/academy and enter code: 927847

The mental components of test anxiety include trouble focusing and inability to remember learned information. During a test, your mind is on high alert, which can help you recall information and stay focused for an extended period of time. However, anxiety interferes with your mind's natural processes, causing you to blank out, even on the questions you know well. The strain of testing during anxiety makes it difficult to stay focused, especially on a test that may take several hours. Extreme anxiety can take a huge mental toll, making it difficult not only to recall test information but even to understand the test questions or pull your thoughts together.

Review Video: How Test Anxiety Affects Memory
Visit mometrix.com/academy and enter code: 609003

Effects of Test Anxiety

Test anxiety is like a disease—if left untreated, it will get progressively worse. Anxiety leads to poor performance, and this reinforces the feelings of fear and failure, which in turn lead to poor performances on subsequent tests. It can grow from a mild nervousness to a crippling condition. If allowed to progress, test anxiety can have a big impact on your schooling, and consequently on your future.

Test anxiety can spread to other parts of your life. Anxiety on tests can become anxiety in any stressful situation, and blanking on a test can turn into panicking in a job situation. But fortunately, you don't have to let anxiety rule your testing and determine your grades. There are a number of relatively simple steps you can take to move past anxiety and function normally on a test and in the rest of life.

Review Video: How Test Anxiety Impacts Your Grades
Visit mometrix.com/academy and enter code: 939819

Physical Steps for Beating Test Anxiety

While test anxiety is a serious problem, the good news is that it can be overcome. It doesn't have to control your ability to think and remember information. While it may take time, you can begin taking steps today to beat anxiety.

Just as your first hint that you may be struggling with anxiety comes from the physical symptoms, the first step to treating it is also physical. Rest is crucial for having a clear, strong mind. If you are tired, it is much easier to give in to anxiety. But if you establish good sleep habits, your body and mind will be ready to perform optimally, without the strain of exhaustion. Additionally, sleeping well helps you to retain information better, so you're more likely to recall the answers when you see the test questions.

Getting good sleep means more than going to bed on time. It's important to allow your brain time to relax. Take study breaks from time to time so it doesn't get overworked, and don't study right before bed. Take time to rest your mind before trying to rest your body, or you may find it difficult to fall asleep.

Review Video: The Importance of Sleep for Your Brain
Visit mometrix.com/academy and enter code: 319338

Along with sleep, other aspects of physical health are important in preparing for a test. Good nutrition is vital for good brain function. Sugary foods and drinks may give a burst of energy but this burst is followed by a crash, both physically and emotionally. Instead, fuel your body with protein and vitamin-rich foods.

Also, drink plenty of water. Dehydration can lead to headaches and exhaustion, especially if your brain is already under stress from the rigors of the test. Particularly if your test is a long one, drink water during the breaks. And if possible, take an energy-boosting snack to eat between sections.

Review Video: How Diet Can Affect your Mood
Visit mometrix.com/academy and enter code: 624317

Along with sleep and diet, a third important part of physical health is exercise. Maintaining a steady workout schedule is helpful, but even taking 5-minute study breaks to walk can help get your blood pumping faster and clear your head. Exercise also releases endorphins, which contribute to a positive feeling and can help combat test anxiety.

When you nurture your physical health, you are also contributing to your mental health. If your body is healthy, your mind is much more likely to be healthy as well. So take time to rest, nourish your body with healthy food and water, and get moving as much as possible. Taking these physical steps will make you stronger and more able to take the mental steps necessary to overcome test anxiety.

Review Video: How to Stay Healthy and Prevent Test Anxiety
Visit mometrix.com/academy and enter code: 877894

Mental Steps for Beating Test Anxiety

Working on the mental side of test anxiety can be more challenging, but as with the physical side, there are clear steps you can take to overcome it. As mentioned earlier, test anxiety often stems from lack of preparation, so the obvious solution is to prepare for the test. Effective studying may be the most important weapon you have for beating test anxiety, but you can and should employ several other mental tools to combat fear.

First, boost your confidence by reminding yourself of past success—tests or projects that you aced. If you're putting as much effort into preparing for this test as you did for those, there's no reason you should expect to fail here. Work hard to prepare; then trust your preparation.

Second, surround yourself with encouraging people. It can be helpful to find a study group, but be sure that the people you're around will encourage a positive attitude. If you spend time with others who are anxious or cynical, this will only contribute to your own anxiety. Look for others who are motivated to study hard from a desire to succeed, not from a fear of failure.

Third, reward yourself. A test is physically and mentally tiring, even without anxiety, and it can be helpful to have something to look forward to. Plan an activity following the test, regardless of the outcome, such as going to a movie or getting ice cream.

When you are taking the test, if you find yourself beginning to feel anxious, remind yourself that you know the material. Visualize successfully completing the test. Then take a few deep, relaxing breaths and return to it. Work through the questions carefully but with confidence, knowing that you are capable of succeeding.

Developing a healthy mental approach to test taking will also aid in other areas of life. Test anxiety affects more than just the actual test—it can be damaging to your mental health and even contribute to depression. It's important to beat test anxiety before it becomes a problem for more than testing.

Review Video: Test Anxiety and Depression
Visit mometrix.com/academy and enter code: 904704

Study Strategy

Being prepared for the test is necessary to combat anxiety, but what does being prepared look like? You may study for hours on end and still not feel prepared. What you need is a strategy for test prep. The next few pages outline our recommended steps to help you plan out and conquer the challenge of preparation.

STEP 1: SCOPE OUT THE TEST

Learn everything you can about the format (multiple choice, essay, etc.) and what will be on the test. Gather any study materials, course outlines, or sample exams that may be available. Not only will this help you to prepare, but knowing what to expect can help to alleviate test anxiety.

STEP 2: MAP OUT THE MATERIAL

Look through the textbook or study guide and make note of how many chapters or sections it has. Then divide these over the time you have. For example, if a book has 15 chapters and you have five days to study, you need to cover three chapters each day. Even better, if you have the time, leave an extra day at the end for overall review after you have gone through the material in depth.

If time is limited, you may need to prioritize the material. Look through it and make note of which sections you think you already have a good grasp on, and which need review. While you are studying, skim quickly through the familiar sections and take more time on the challenging parts. Write out your plan so you don't get lost as you go. Having a written plan also helps you feel more in control of the study, so anxiety is less likely to arise from feeling overwhelmed at the amount to cover.

STEP 3: GATHER YOUR TOOLS

Decide what study method works best for you. Do you prefer to highlight in the book as you study and then go back over the highlighted portions? Or do you type out notes of the important information? Or is it helpful to make flashcards that you can carry with you? Assemble the pens, index cards, highlighters, post-it notes, and any other materials you may need so you won't be distracted by getting up to find things while you study.

If you're having a hard time retaining the information or organizing your notes, experiment with different methods. For example, try color-coding by subject with colored pens, highlighters, or post-it notes. If you learn better by hearing, try recording yourself reading your notes so you can listen while in the car, working out, or simply sitting at your desk. Ask a friend to quiz you from your flashcards, or try teaching someone the material to solidify it in your mind.

STEP 4: CREATE YOUR ENVIRONMENT

It's important to avoid distractions while you study. This includes both the obvious distractions like visitors and the subtle distractions like an uncomfortable chair (or a too-comfortable couch that makes you want to fall asleep). Set up the best study environment possible: good lighting and a comfortable work area. If background music helps you focus, you may want to turn it on, but otherwise keep the room quiet. If you are using a computer to take notes, be sure you don't have any other windows open, especially applications like social media, games, or anything else that could distract you. Silence your phone and turn off notifications. Be sure to keep water close by so you stay hydrated while you study (but avoid unhealthy drinks and snacks).

Also, take into account the best time of day to study. Are you freshest first thing in the morning? Try to set aside some time then to work through the material. Is your mind clearer in the afternoon or evening? Schedule your study session then. Another method is to study at the same time of day that you will take the test, so that your brain gets used to working on the material at that time and will be ready to focus at test time.

STEP 5: STUDY!

Once you have done all the study preparation, it's time to settle into the actual studying. Sit down, take a few moments to settle your mind so you can focus, and begin to follow your study plan. Don't give in to distractions or let yourself procrastinate. This is your time to prepare so you'll be ready to fearlessly approach the test. Make the most of the time and stay focused.

Of course, you don't want to burn out. If you study too long you may find that you're not retaining the information very well. Take regular study breaks. For example, taking five minutes out of every hour to walk briskly, breathing deeply and swinging your arms, can help your mind stay fresh.

As you get to the end of each chapter or section, it's a good idea to do a quick review. Remind yourself of what you learned and work on any difficult parts. When you feel that you've mastered the material, move on to the next part. At the end of your study session, briefly skim through your notes again.

But while review is helpful, cramming last minute is NOT. If at all possible, work ahead so that you won't need to fit all your study into the last day. Cramming overloads your brain with more information than it can process and retain, and your tired mind may struggle to recall even previously learned information when it is overwhelmed with last-minute study. Also, the urgent nature of cramming and the stress placed on your brain contribute to anxiety. You'll be more likely to go to the test feeling unprepared and having trouble thinking clearly.

So don't cram, and don't stay up late before the test, even just to review your notes at a leisurely pace. Your brain needs rest more than it needs to go over the information again. In fact, plan to finish your studies by noon or early afternoon the day before the test. Give your brain the rest of the day to relax or focus on other things, and get a good night's sleep. Then you will be fresh for the test and better able to recall what you've studied.

STEP 6: TAKE A PRACTICE TEST

Many courses offer sample tests, either online or in the study materials. This is an excellent resource to check whether you have mastered the material, as well as to prepare for the test format and environment.

Check the test format ahead of time: the number of questions, the type (multiple choice, free response, etc.), and the time limit. Then create a plan for working through them. For example, if you have 30 minutes to take a 60-question test, your limit is 30 seconds per question. Spend less time on the questions you know well so that you can take more time on the difficult ones.

If you have time to take several practice tests, take the first one open book, with no time limit. Work through the questions at your own pace and make sure you fully understand them. Gradually work up to taking a test under test conditions: sit at a desk with all study materials put away and set a timer. Pace yourself to make sure you finish the test with time to spare and go back to check your answers if you have time.

After each test, check your answers. On the questions you missed, be sure you understand why you missed them. Did you misread the question (tests can use tricky wording)? Did you forget the information? Or was it something you hadn't learned? Go back and study any shaky areas that the practice tests reveal.

Taking these tests not only helps with your grade, but also aids in combating test anxiety. If you're already used to the test conditions, you're less likely to worry about it, and working through tests until you're scoring well gives you a confidence boost. Go through the practice tests until you feel comfortable, and then you can go into the test knowing that you're ready for it.

Test Tips

On test day, you should be confident, knowing that you've prepared well and are ready to answer the questions. But aside from preparation, there are several test day strategies you can employ to maximize your performance.

First, as stated before, get a good night's sleep the night before the test (and for several nights before that, if possible). Go into the test with a fresh, alert mind rather than staying up late to study.

Try not to change too much about your normal routine on the day of the test. It's important to eat a nutritious breakfast, but if you normally don't eat breakfast at all, consider eating just a protein bar. If you're a coffee drinker, go ahead and have your normal coffee. Just make sure you time it so that the caffeine doesn't wear off right in the middle of your test. Avoid sugary beverages, and drink enough water to stay hydrated but not so much that you need a restroom break 10 minutes into the test. If your test isn't first thing in the morning, consider going for a walk or doing a light workout before the test to get your blood flowing.

Allow yourself enough time to get ready, and leave for the test with plenty of time to spare so you won't have the anxiety of scrambling to arrive in time. Another reason to be early is to select a good seat. It's helpful to sit away from doors and windows, which can be distracting. Find a good seat, get out your supplies, and settle your mind before the test begins.

When the test begins, start by going over the instructions carefully, even if you already know what to expect. Make sure you avoid any careless mistakes by following the directions.

Then begin working through the questions, pacing yourself as you've practiced. If you're not sure on an answer, don't spend too much time on it, and don't let it shake your confidence. Either skip it and come back later, or eliminate as many wrong answers as possible and guess among the remaining ones. Don't dwell on these questions as you continue—put them out of your mind and focus on what lies ahead.

Be sure to read all of the answer choices, even if you're sure the first one is the right answer. Sometimes you'll find a better one if you keep reading. But don't second-guess yourself if you do immediately know the answer. Your gut instinct is usually right. Don't let test anxiety rob you of the information you know.

If you have time at the end of the test (and if the test format allows), go back and review your answers. Be cautious about changing any, since your first instinct tends to be correct, but make sure you didn't misread any of the questions or accidentally mark the wrong answer choice. Look over any you skipped and make an educated guess.

At the end, leave the test feeling confident. You've done your best, so don't waste time worrying about your performance or wishing you could change anything. Instead, celebrate the successful

completion of this test. And finally, use this test to learn how to deal with anxiety even better next time.

Important Qualification

Not all anxiety is created equal. If your test anxiety is causing major issues in your life beyond the classroom or testing center, or if you are experiencing troubling physical symptoms related to your anxiety, it may be a sign of a serious physiological or psychological condition. If this sounds like your situation, we strongly encourage you to seek professional help.

How to Overcome Your Fear of Math

The word *math* is enough to strike fear into most hearts. How many of us have memories of sitting through confusing lectures, wrestling over mind-numbing homework, or taking tests that still seem incomprehensible even after hours of study? Years after graduation, many still shudder at these memories.

The fact is, math is not just a classroom subject. It has real-world implications that you face every day, whether you realize it or not. This may be balancing your monthly budget, deciding how many supplies to buy for a project, or simply splitting a meal check with friends. The idea of daily confrontations with math can be so paralyzing that some develop a condition known as *math anxiety*.

But you do NOT need to be paralyzed by this anxiety! In fact, while you may have thought all your life that you're not good at math, or that your brain isn't wired to understand it, the truth is that you may have been conditioned to think this way. From your earliest school days, the way you were taught affected the way you viewed different subjects. And the way math has been taught has changed.

Several decades ago, there was a shift in American math classrooms. The focus changed from traditional problem-solving to a conceptual view of topics, de-emphasizing the importance of learning the basics and building on them. The solid foundation necessary for math progression and confidence was undermined. Math became more of a vague concept than a concrete idea. Today, it is common to think of math, not as a straightforward system, but as a mysterious, complicated method that can't be fully understood unless you're a genius.

This is why you may still have nightmares about being called on to answer a difficult problem in front of the class. Math anxiety is a very real, though unnecessary, fear.

Math anxiety may begin with a single class period. Let's say you missed a day in 6th grade math and never quite understood the concept that was taught while you were gone. Since math is cumulative, with each new concept building on past ones, this could very well affect the rest of your math career. Without that one day's knowledge, it will be difficult to understand any other concepts that link to it. Rather than realizing that you're just missing one key piece, you may begin to believe that you're simply not capable of understanding math.

This belief can change the way you approach other classes, career options, and everyday life experiences, if you become anxious at the thought that math might be required. A student who loves science may choose a different path of study upon realizing that multiple math classes will be required for a degree. An aspiring medical student may hesitate at the thought of going through the necessary math classes. For some this anxiety escalates into a more extreme state known as *math phobia*.

Math anxiety is challenging to address because it is rooted deeply and may come from a variety of causes: an embarrassing moment in class, a teacher who did not explain concepts well and contributed to a shaky foundation, or a failed test that contributed to the belief of math failure.

These causes add up over time, encouraged by society's popular view that math is hard and unpleasant. Eventually a person comes to firmly believe that he or she is simply bad at math. This belief makes it difficult to grasp new concepts or even remember old ones. Homework and test grades begin to slip, which only confirms the belief. The poor performance is not due to lack of ability but is caused by math anxiety.

Math anxiety is an emotional issue, not a lack of intelligence. But when it becomes deeply rooted, it can become more than just an emotional problem. Physical symptoms appear. Blood pressure may rise and heartbeat may quicken at the sight of a math problem – or even the thought of math! This fear leads to a mental block. When someone with math anxiety is asked to perform a calculation, even a basic problem can seem overwhelming and impossible. The emotional and physical response to the thought of math prevents the brain from working through it logically.

The more this happens, the more a person's confidence drops, and the more math anxiety is generated. This vicious cycle must be broken!

The first step in breaking the cycle is to go back to very beginning and make sure you really understand the basics of how math works and why it works. It is not enough to memorize rules for multiplication and division. If you don't know WHY these rules work, your foundation will be shaky and you will be at risk of developing a phobia. Understanding mathematical concepts not only promotes confidence and security, but allows you to build on this understanding for new concepts. Additionally, you can solve unfamiliar problems using familiar concepts and processes.

Why is it that students in other countries regularly outperform American students in math? The answer likely boils down to a couple of things: the foundation of mathematical conceptual understanding and societal perception. While students in the US are not expected to *like* or *get* math, in many other nations, students are expected not only to understand math but also to excel at it.

Changing the American view of math that leads to math anxiety is a monumental task. It requires changing the training of teachers nationwide, from kindergarten through high school, so that they learn to teach the *why* behind math and to combat the wrong math views that students may develop. It also involves changing the stigma associated with math, so that it is no longer viewed as unpleasant and incomprehensible. While these are necessary changes, they are challenging and will take time. But in the meantime, math anxiety is not irreversible—it can be faced and defeated, one person at a time.

False Beliefs

One reason math anxiety has taken such hold is that several false beliefs have been created and shared until they became widely accepted. Some of these unhelpful beliefs include the following:

There is only one way to solve a math problem. In the same way that you can choose from different driving routes and still arrive at the same house, you can solve a math problem using different methods and still find the correct answer. A person who understands the reasoning behind math calculations may be able to look at an unfamiliar concept and find the right answer, just by applying logic to the knowledge they already have. This approach may be different than what is taught in the classroom, but it is still valid. Unfortunately, even many teachers view math as a subject where the best course of action is to memorize the rule or process for each problem rather than as a place for students to exercise logic and creativity in finding a solution.

Many people don't have a mind for math. A person who has struggled due to poor teaching or math anxiety may falsely believe that he or she doesn't have the mental capacity to grasp mathematical concepts. Most of the time, this is false. Many people find that when they are relieved of their math anxiety, they have more than enough brainpower to understand math.

Men are naturally better at math than women. Even though research has shown this to be false, many young women still avoid math careers and classes because of their belief that their math abilities are inferior. Many girls have come to believe that math is a male skill and have given up trying to understand or enjoy it.

Counting aids are bad. Something like counting on your fingers or drawing out a problem to visualize it may be frowned on as childish or a crutch, but these devices can help you get a tangible understanding of a problem or a concept.

Sadly, many students buy into these ideologies at an early age. A young girl who enjoys math class may be conditioned to think that she doesn't actually have the brain for it because math is for boys, and may turn her energies to other pursuits, permanently closing the door on a wide range of opportunities. A child who finds the right answer but doesn't follow the teacher's method may believe that he is doing it wrong and isn't good at math. A student who never had a problem with math before may have a poor teacher and become confused, yet believe that the problem is because she doesn't have a mathematical mind.

Students who have bought into these erroneous beliefs quickly begin to add their own anxieties, adapting them to their own personal situations:

I'll never use this in real life. A huge number of people wrongly believe that math is irrelevant outside the classroom. By adopting this mindset, they are handicapping themselves for a life in a mathematical world, as well as limiting their career choices. When they are inevitably faced with real-world math, they are conditioning themselves to respond with anxiety.

I'm not quick enough. While timed tests and quizzes, or even simply comparing yourself with other students in the class, can lead to this belief, speed is not an indicator of skill level. A person can work very slowly yet understand at a deep level.

If I can understand it, it's too easy. People with a low view of their own abilities tend to think that if they are able to grasp a concept, it must be simple. They cannot accept the idea that they are capable of understanding math. This belief will make it harder to learn, no matter how intelligent they are.

I just can't learn this. An overwhelming number of people think this, from young children to adults, and much of the time it is simply not true. But this mindset can turn into a self-fulfilling prophecy that keeps you from exercising and growing your math ability.

The good news is, each of these myths can be debunked. For most people, they are based on emotion and psychology, NOT on actual ability! It will take time, effort, and the desire to change, but change is possible. Even if you have spent years thinking that you don't have the capability to understand math, it is not too late to uncover your true ability and find relief from the anxiety that surrounds math.

Math Strategies

It is important to have a plan of attack to combat math anxiety. There are many useful strategies for pinpointing the fears or myths and eradicating them:

Go back to the basics. For most people, math anxiety stems from a poor foundation. You may think that you have a complete understanding of addition and subtraction, or even decimals and percentages, but make absolutely sure. Learning math is different from learning other subjects. For example, when you learn history, you study various time periods and places and events. It may be important to memorize dates or find out about the lives of famous people. When you move from US history to world history, there will be some overlap, but a large amount of the information will be new. Mathematical concepts, on the other hand, are very closely linked and highly dependent on each other. It's like climbing a ladder – if a rung is missing from your understanding, it may be difficult or impossible for you to climb any higher, no matter how hard you try. So go back and make sure your math foundation is strong. This may mean taking a remedial math course, going to a tutor to work through the shaky concepts, or just going through your old homework to make sure you really understand it.

Speak the language. Math has a large vocabulary of terms and phrases unique to working problems. Sometimes these are completely new terms, and sometimes they are common words, but are used differently in a math setting. If you can't speak the language, it will be very difficult to get a thorough understanding of the concepts. It's common for students to think that they don't understand math when they simply don't understand the vocabulary. The good news is that this is fairly easy to fix. Brushing up on any terms you aren't quite sure of can help bring the rest of the concepts into focus.

Check your anxiety level. When you think about math, do you feel nervous or uncomfortable? Do you struggle with feelings of inadequacy, even on concepts that you know you've already learned? It's important to understand your specific math anxieties, and what triggers them. When you catch yourself falling back on a false belief, mentally replace it with the truth. Don't let yourself believe that you can't learn, or that struggling with a concept means you'll never understand it. Instead, remind yourself of how much you've already learned and dwell on that past success. Visualize grasping the new concept, linking it to your old knowledge, and moving on to the next challenge. Also, learn how to manage anxiety when it arises. There are many techniques for coping with the irrational fears that rise to the surface when you enter the math classroom. This may include controlled breathing, replacing negative thoughts with positive ones, or visualizing success. Anxiety interferes with your ability to concentrate and absorb information, which in turn contributes to greater anxiety. If you can learn how to regain control of your thinking, you will be better able to pay attention, make progress, and succeed!

Don't go it alone. Like any deeply ingrained belief, math anxiety is not easy to eradicate. And there is no need for you to wrestle through it on your own. It will take time, and many people find that speaking with a counselor or psychiatrist helps. They can help you develop strategies for responding to anxiety and overcoming old ideas. Additionally, it can be very helpful to take a short course or seek out a math tutor to help you find and fix the missing rungs on your ladder and make sure that you're ready to progress to the next level. You can also find a number of math aids online: courses that will teach you mental devices for figuring out problems, how to get the most out of your math classes, etc.

Check your math attitude. No matter how much you want to learn and overcome your anxiety, you'll have trouble if you still have a negative attitude toward math. If you think it's too hard, or just have general feelings of dread about math, it will be hard to learn and to break through the anxiety. Work on cultivating a positive math attitude. Remind yourself that math is not just a hurdle to be cleared, but a valuable asset. When you view math with a positive attitude, you'll be much more likely to understand and even enjoy it. This is something you must do for yourself. You may find it helpful to visit with a counselor. Your tutor, friends, and family may cheer you on in your endeavors. But your greatest asset is yourself. You are inside your own mind – tell yourself what you need to hear. Relive past victories. Remind yourself that you are capable of understanding math. Root out any false beliefs that linger and replace them with positive truths. Even if it doesn't feel true at first, it will begin to affect your thinking and pave the way for a positive, anxiety-free mindset.

Aside from these general strategies, there are a number of specific practical things you can do to begin your journey toward overcoming math anxiety. Something as simple as learning a new note-taking strategy can change the way you approach math and give you more confidence and understanding. New study techniques can also make a huge difference.

Math anxiety leads to bad habits. If it causes you to be afraid of answering a question in class, you may gravitate toward the back row. You may be embarrassed to ask for help. And you may procrastinate on assignments, which leads to rushing through them at the last moment when it's too late to get a better understanding. It's important to identify your negative behaviors and replace them with positive ones:

Prepare ahead of time. Read the lesson before you go to class. Being exposed to the topics that will be covered in class ahead of time, even if you don't understand them perfectly, is extremely helpful in increasing what you retain from the lecture. Do your homework and, if you're still shaky, go over some extra problems. The key to a solid understanding of math is practice.

Sit front and center. When you can easily see and hear, you'll understand more, and you'll avoid the distractions of other students if no one is in front of you. Plus, you're more likely to be sitting with students who are positive and engaged, rather than others with math anxiety. Let their positive math attitude rub off on you.

Ask questions in class and out. If you don't understand something, just ask. If you need a more in-depth explanation, the teacher may need to work with you outside of class, but often it's a simple concept you don't quite understand, and a single question may clear it up. If you wait, you may not be able to follow the rest of the day's lesson. For extra help, most professors have office hours outside of class when you can go over concepts one-on-one to clear up any uncertainties. Additionally, there may be a *math lab* or study session you can attend for homework help. Take advantage of this.

Review. Even if you feel that you've fully mastered a concept, review it periodically to reinforce it. Going over an old lesson has several benefits: solidifying your understanding, giving you a confidence boost, and even giving some new insights into material that you're currently learning! Don't let yourself get rusty. That can lead to problems with learning later concepts.

Teaching Tips

While the math student's mindset is the most crucial to overcoming math anxiety, it is also important for others to adjust their math attitudes. Teachers and parents have an enormous influence on how students relate to math. They can either contribute to math confidence or math anxiety.

As a parent or teacher, it is very important to convey a positive math attitude. Retelling horror stories of your own bad experience with math will contribute to a new generation of math anxiety. Even if you don't share your experiences, others will be able to sense your fears and may begin to believe them.

Even a careless comment can have a big impact, so watch for phrases like *He's not good at math* or *I never liked math.* You are a crucial role model, and your children or students will unconsciously adopt your mindset. Give them a positive example to follow. Rather than teaching them to fear the math world before they even know it, teach them about all its potential and excitement.

Work to present math as an integral, beautiful, and understandable part of life. Encourage creativity in solving problems. Watch for false beliefs and dispel them. Cross the lines between subjects: integrate history, English, and music with math. Show students how math is used every day, and how the entire world is based on mathematical principles, from the pull of gravity to the shape of seashells. Instead of letting students see math as a necessary evil, direct them to view it as an imaginative, beautiful art form – an art form that they are capable of mastering and using.

Don't give too narrow a view of math. It is more than just numbers. Yes, working problems and learning formulas is a large part of classroom math. But don't let the teaching stop there. Teach students about the everyday implications of math. Show them how nature works according to the laws of mathematics, and take them outside to make discoveries of their own. Expose them to math-related careers by inviting visiting speakers, asking students to do research and presentations, and learning students' interests and aptitudes on a personal level.

Demonstrate the importance of math. Many people see math as nothing more than a required stepping stone to their degree, a nuisance with no real usefulness. Teach students that algebra is used every day in managing their bank accounts, in following recipes, and in scheduling the day's events. Show them how learning to do geometric proofs helps them to develop logical thinking, an invaluable life skill. Let them see that math surrounds them and is integrally linked to their daily lives: that weather predictions are based on math, that math was used to design cars and other machines, etc. Most of all, give them the tools to use math to enrich their lives.

Make math as tangible as possible. Use visual aids and objects that can be touched. It is much easier to grasp a concept when you can hold it in your hands and manipulate it, rather than just listening to the lecture. Encourage math outside of the classroom. The real world is full of measuring, counting, and calculating, so let students participate in this. Keep your eyes open for numbers and patterns to discuss. Talk about how scores are calculated in sports games and how far apart plants are placed in a garden row for maximum growth. Build the mindset that math is a normal and interesting part of daily life.

Finally, find math resources that help to build a positive math attitude. There are a number of books that show math as fascinating and exciting while teaching important concepts, for example: *The Math Curse; A Wrinkle in Time; The Phantom Tollbooth;* and *Fractals, Googols and Other Mathematical Tales.* You can also find a number of online resources: math puzzles and games, videos that show math in nature, and communities of math enthusiasts. On a local level, students can compete in a variety of math competitions with other schools or join a math club.

The student who experiences math as exciting and interesting is unlikely to suffer from math anxiety. Going through life without this handicap is an immense advantage and opens many doors that others have closed through their fear.

Self-Check

Whether you suffer from math anxiety or not, chances are that you have been exposed to some of the false beliefs mentioned above. Now is the time to check yourself for any errors you may have accepted. Do you think you're not wired for math? Or that you don't need to understand it since you're not planning on a math career? Do you think math is just too difficult for the average person?

Find the errors you've taken to heart and replace them with positive thinking. Are you capable of learning math? Yes! Can you control your anxiety? Yes! These errors will resurface from time to time, so be watchful. Don't let others with math anxiety influence you or sway your confidence. If you're having trouble with a concept, find help. Don't let it discourage you!

Create a plan of attack for defeating math anxiety and sharpening your skills. Do some research and decide if it would help you to take a class, get a tutor, or find some online resources to fine-tune your knowledge. Make the effort to get good nutrition, hydration, and sleep so that you are operating at full capacity. Remind yourself daily that you are skilled and that anxiety does not control you. Your mind is capable of so much more than you know. Give it the tools it needs to grow and thrive.

Thank You

We at Mometrix would like to extend our heartfelt thanks to you, our friend and patron, for allowing us to play a part in your journey. It is a privilege to serve people from all walks of life who are unified in their commitment to building the best future they can for themselves.

The preparation you devote to these important testing milestones may be the most valuable educational opportunity you have for making a real difference in your life. We encourage you to put your heart into it—that feeling of succeeding, overcoming, and yes, conquering will be well worth the hours you've invested.

We want to hear your story, your struggles and your successes, and if you see any opportunities for us to improve our materials so we can help others even more effectively in the future, please share that with us as well. **The team at Mometrix would be absolutely thrilled to hear from you!** So please, send us an email (support@mometrix.com) and let's stay in touch.

> **If you'd like some additional help, check out these other resources we offer for your exam:**
> **http://MometrixFlashcards.com/ACCUPLACER**

Additional Bonus Material

Due to our efforts to try to keep this book to a manageable length, we've created a link that will give you access to all of your additional bonus material.

Please visit http://www.mometrix.com/bonus948/accuplacer
to access the information.

143

144

Made in the USA
Columbia, SC
12 October 2022

69343869R00085